NEHEMIAH

CYRIL J. BARBER

LOIZEAUX BROTHERS
Neptune, New Jersey

Dedicated to
DR. HOWARD G. HENDRICKS
Bible teacher *par excellence*
who first taught me how to study the Bible
and to my sons
ALLAN and STEPHEN
who, in our study of the Word together,
share with me in the joy of discovery

❧❧

Nehemiah and the Dynamics of Effective Leadership
First Edition, September 1976
Revised Edition, July 1991

© 1976 by Loizeaux Brothers, Inc.
© 1991 by Cyril J. Barber

A Publication of Loizeaux Brothers, Inc.
*A Nonprofit Organization Devoted to the Lord's Work
and to the Spread of His Truth*

Unless otherwise indicated, the translations or paraphrases
of Scripture quoted in this book are the author's.

Library of Congress Cataloging in Publication Data

Barber, Cyril J.
Nehemiah and the dynamics of effective leadership / Cyril J.
Barber. — Rev. ed.
Includes bibliographical references.
ISBN 0-87213-026-6
1. Bible. O.T. Nehemiah—Criticism, interpretation, etc.
2. Nehemiah (Governor of Judah) 3. Leadership—Biblical teaching.
I. Title.
BS1365.2.B37   1991
222'.806—dc20   91-21697

Printed in the United States of America

10   9   8   7   6   5   4   3   2

CONTENTS

3

PREFACE

Early in my career I was thrust into a position of administrative responsibility for which I was ill prepared. Somehow the subjects I was required to master for my degree in accountancy never included the basic principles of personnel leadership. This, of course, was in the days before "curriculum revision" became the bane of educational institutions. It was also prior to Argyris and Drucker, Fiedler and Likert, Montgomery and Stogdill putting into print all they had learned from their years of experience. Only after changing professions twenty years later did I take my first course in administration.

In the period of time which intervened between beginning my professional career and making this change I had a lot to learn And I made a lot of mistakes! Fortunately I found in the book of Nehemiah what I needed, namely guidance on how to handle the administrative problems of everyday life. In fact, Nehemiah's "Memoirs" were so intriguing that I made a special point of studying them at least once each year.

In the course of time I met other people in similar situations. Seminarians had become pastors and needed suggestions on how to work with their church board. Mechanics had been made foremen and now had to handle "paper work." Engineers had "graduated" from the construction site to an office desk and needed guidance in public relations. Clerks had been made department heads and were in need of counsel on how to supervise personnel. And missionaries had become field superintendents—all, at times, with disastrous results.

I first began sharing insights from Nehemiah with church groups of businessmen and women about fifteen years ago. These informal studies were later expanded to include ministers' seminars and missionary retreats in the United States and Canada, as well as popular expository addresses to those preparing for the ministry in Bible colleges and seminaries.

This book is the outgrowth of these encounters. It seeks to present in a very simple way the principles which I have found to be so beneficial in my own life.

I trust that this material will encourage others to dig into the Scriptures for themselves, for there is no substitute for a personal exposure to the Word of God!

In preparing the manuscript for publication I am obviously in debt to those who have so graciously given of their time in typing and proofreading these pages. Theirs has indeed been a labor of love! I am also indebted to Dr. Howard G. Hendricks of Dallas Seminary for his lectures on Bible Analysis. What I learned under his capable guidance continues to be a tremendous influence in my own life. Furthermore, I wish to express my sincere thanks to Robert Barneson of Flour Engineers and Contractors, Los Angeles, and to Dr. Robert D. Culver of the First Evangelical Free Church, Lincoln, Nebraska, for their kindness in reading the manuscript and offering many helpful suggestions.

CYRIL J. BARBER

Rosemead Graduate School of Psychology
Rosemead, California

INTRODUCTION

WHERE IT'S AT!

Nehemiah 1:1-4

While addressing a group of businessmen on the subject of leadership, a prominent industrialist pointed out that *"human history is a record of mass accomplishment under leadership."*
As we reflect on this observation we find that in our churches and on the mission field, in education and in commerce, in politics and in medicine, we are dependent upon leaders. However, we must ask and answer certain basic questions about leadership. For example: What is its basis? How may leaders develop their full potential? What steps can be taken to conserve the results of their successes? How may leaders take inventory of their present progress and prepare for the challenges of the future?
There are many prescriptions for successful leadership. Each person, it seems, has his own. The seemingly endless variety is confusing. Let me tell you how I stumbled onto the solution.
I came to know the Lord Jesus Christ as my Saviour during my second year in business. This encounter completely changed my life. Early in my experience I realized the need to put Christ first in my life. In addition, I learned that if I was to grow spiritually I would need to study the Bible for myself. As I began examining the Scriptures, I found that God has communicated to us the things which we need to know about this secular existence of ours as well as a life of godliness (2 Peter 1:3-4). I also learned that each book of the Bible has a specific purpose. For example, God has explained the place and importance of human relationships in the book of Proverbs. He has given us a blueprint for marital adjustment in the Song of

Solomon. He has shown us how to live in the midst of spiritual decline in Second Timothy. He has described the way in which we may maintain fellowship with Him in John's first Epistle.

But what is there in the Bible for those thrust into positions of leadership?

It was Dr. V. Raymond Edman who, in *The Disciplines of Life*, first directed my attention to the book of Nehemiah. In this book I found what I had been looking for! Here were the specific principles I needed. From the book of Nehemiah I learned how to *plan* my work, *organize* my time and resources, *integrate* my duties into the total operation of the company, *motivate* others, and *measure* the results. I learned the importance of setting realistic goals, and found out what to do before I reached my objectives.

As I studied the book I learned, to my amazement, that God has anticipated the problems of those in middle-management. He has also shown us how to handle opposition. He has explained the difference between the "task leader" and a "social-emotional specialist." He has illustrated for us what we should do when we take over a new job. He has given us an example of the way we should conduct ourselves in delicate, trying situations. And most important of all, He has demonstrated the importance and practical value of religious convictions in effective administration.

From the time I first read *The Disciplines of Life* in 1948 to the present, I have made a point of studying the book of Nehemiah once each year. This has been done for the purpose of refreshing my own mind on the important information contained in these "Memoirs." Continued exposure to the wealth of material found in this book has helped me to take constant inventory of the quality of my own work, objectives, and relationships. I have found this portion of God's Word to be an amazing and perceptive commentary on the Apostle Paul's statement: "And whatever you do in word or deed, do all in the name of the Lord Jesus . . . [in fact] whatever you do, do it heartily as unto the Lord" (Colossians 3:17-23).

Problem Number One

The first problem we face as we begin to look into the book of

Nehemiah is one of interpretation. Some of the first expositions I read on Nehemiah spiritualized the text. The writers were faced with the fact that the book of Nehemiah is in the Old Testament and, as such, deals with Israel and not with the Church. They felt under an obligation to make the Old Testament meaningful to Christians. To do this they looked for spiritual principles which could be applied to the Church collectively and believers individually. Theirs is the *allegorical* method of interpretation.

There are problems with this kind of interpretation. As Bernard Ramm pointed out, "The Bible treated allegorically becomes putty in the hand of the exegete. Different doctrinal systems could emerge within the framework of allegorical hermeneutics [i.e., interpretation] and no way would exist to determine which were the true one. . . . The allegorical method puts a premium on the subjective and the doleful result is the obscuration of the Word of God."[1]

Our approach will *not* be to escape Judaism by spiritualizing what Nehemiah has written. We will follow a normal, consistent, literal interpretation of the text. After all, Nehemiah was a real person. He faced real problems. And he built a real wall. We will include in our interpretation relevant information contained in the historic setting, the geographic situation, and the cultural background of the people. By following the "basic, customary, social designation" of what Nehemiah saw fit to record, we will be able accurately to interpret what we read. Then, instead of looking for secondary, spiritual meanings, we will be free to look for *principles*. We will find that these principles are timeless. With them to guide us we will be able to learn more of the dynamics of successful leadership—whether our sphere of service be in the pastorate, on the mission field, in a corporation, or in the halls of government.

Meet the Courtier

But what of Nehemiah? Who was he? When and where did he live? And what did he do?

Nehemiah was probably from the tribe of Judah (see

[1] Bernard Ramm, *Protestant Biblical Interpretation* (Grand Rapids: Baker, 1970), pp. 30-31.

Nehemiah 1:2; 2:3; 7:2), and he may even have been a descendant of King David (see Nehemiah 1:4 and 1 Chronicles 3:19). He introduces himself to us as "the son of Hachaliah." Nothing is known of his father and we are left to conclude that his father had been taken into captivity when Jerusalem fell to the Babylonians. Nehemiah was probably born in captivity and grew to manhóod surrounded by all the corrupting influences of the ancient Near East.

At the time we meet Nehemiah he is serving as a cupbearer (Nehemiah 1:11) in Susa, the principal palace and winter residence of the king. As a cupbearer, he is in a unique position. He holds the offices of prime minister and master of ceremonies rolled into one. Fear of intrigue and the constant threat of assassination caused a king to lead a relatively lonely life. It was, therefore, quite natural for him to gravitate toward a man of wisdom, discretion, and ability. A cupbearer who had his monarch's interests at heart, and who stayed abreast of the times, could frequently exert great influence upon his sovereign. Besides testing the king's wine, he was also responsible for guarding his sovereign's sleeping quarters.

As Nehemiah begins his story, he tells us of a visit he received from his brother Hanani. "Now it happened in the month of Chislev [November/December] in the twentieth year [of Artaxerxes I, 445 B.C.] while I was in Susa the capital, that Hanani, one of my brothers, he and some men from Judah came; and I asked them concerning the Jews who had escaped and had survived the captivity, and about Jerusalem. And they said to me, 'The remnant there in the province who survived the captivity are in great distress and reproach, and the walls of Jerusalem are broken down and its gates are burned with fire.' "

The information Nehemiah receives is disheartening. All attempts to rebuild the wall have been frustrated (Ezra 4:4-24). He knows that "a city without locked gates and lofty walls is no city at all." It is defenseless and can afford no protection to those within. As a result, few live in the capital (Nehemiah 11:1).

But why were the Jews in such a deplorable condition? What had happened to them since David established the kingdom and Solomon introduced the "golden age"?

History Need Not Be Hateful

The book of Nehemiah occupies an important place on the stage of history. The Hebrew people had once been a powerful force in the Near East. But the kingdom which David established split in two. The ten northern tribes banded together into one kingdom and the two southern tribes joined forces to form another. From this time onward, their fortunes were mixed. Idolatry prevailed. Ultimately (in 722 B.C.) God punished the northern tribes by allowing the Assyrians to over-run them. They were taken captive, deported, and resettled among other nations.

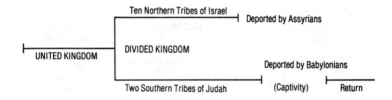

Only Judah survived. The southern tribes, however, failed to learn from Israel's experience. As a result they too were taken captive and deported,[2] this time by the Babylonians (Jeremiah 25:11-12; Daniel 9:2). During the seventy years the Jews spent in captivity, the power of Babylon was broken by the combined forces of the Medes and Persians. Under the new administration, King Cyrus (550-530 B.C.) gave permission for them to return to Palestine and rebuild the Temple (Ezra 1:1-3). The first exiles returned under the leadership of Zerubbabel (538 B.C.; Ezra 1—6). The foundation of the Temple was laid, but the work was opposed by the Samaritans to the north, and more than fifteen years passed before the Temple was completed.

Later on, another group of Jews returned to Jerusalem. They were led by Ezra (458 B.C.; Ezra 7—10). On Ezra's arrival in Palestine, he found the people to be in a deplorable condition—spiritually and morally. He therefore began a widespread teaching ministry (Ezra 7:10). As we shall see, his

[2] The Bible records three successive deportations. These occurred in 605, 597, and 586 B.C.

teaching of the Law would bear fruit fourteen years later (Nehemiah 8—10).

Finally, during the reign of Artaxerxes I Longimanus (465-424 B.C.), Nehemiah returned to Judah. Without a city wall to protect them, the people were constantly being harassed. Morale was low. The rich exploited the poor, and the same sins which had led to the captivity were being practiced once again. Economic depression and spiritual ignorance further accentuated the disunity of the people.

PANORAMA OF EZRA—NEHEMIAH

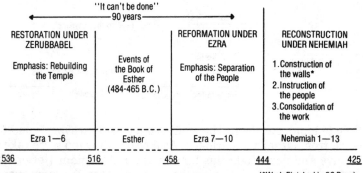

"It can't be done" 90 years			
RESTORATION UNDER ZERUBBABEL		REFORMATION UNDER EZRA	RECONSTRUCTION UNDER NEHEMIAH
Emphasis: Rebuilding the Temple	Events of the Book of Esther (484-465 B.C.)	Emphasis: Separation of the People	1. Construction of the walls* 2. Instruction of the people 3. Consolidation of the work
Ezra 1—6	Esther	Ezra 7—10	Nehemiah 1—13
536	516	458	444 425

(*Work Finished in 52 Days)

The way in which Nehemiah united the people and inspired them to accomplish a seemingly impossible task is most instructive. The strategy he used is fully abreast of the latest motivation research and has been used successfully by businessmen and church leaders through the years.

Synopsis

It will help us understand the scope of Nehemiah's "Memoirs" if we master a basic threefold outline and preview the contents of his book.

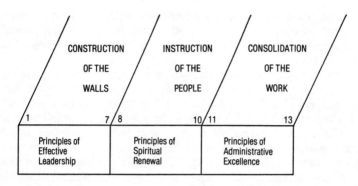

CONSTRUCTION OF THE WALLS | INSTRUCTION OF THE PEOPLE | CONSOLIDATION OF THE WORK

Principles of Effective Leadership | Principles of Spiritual Renewal | Principles of Administrative Excellence

But what of Nehemiah? What was his response to the report brought by Hanani? What led up to his trip to Jerusalem? How did he accomplish what no one else had been able to do?

As soon as Nehemiah learns of conditions in Judah, he immediately begins to intercede on behalf of his brethren (Nehemiah 1:4-11). He shows by his actions that he has a deep concern for them. Four months of intense prayer finally brings the desired answer—but in a way which places him in a very invidious position (2:1-8). His loyalty and tact, however, help him to handle this difficult and potentially dangerous situation, and the king gives permission for him to return to Judah. He journeys to Jerusalem and, on his arrival, quickly assesses the situation. Then he challenges the people with the need to rebuild the wall of their city (2:9-20).

Chapter 3 contains a record of those who volunteered to rebuild the city wall. At first sight it appears to be a dry and uninteresting rehearsal of names. Closer examination reveals that it is permeated with important principles of effective leadership. From this record we might be tempted to conclude that the wall of the city was built without mishap. Actually, the work met with stiff opposition (Nehemiah 4—6). Opposition, however, by its very nature, follows essentially the same pattern regardless of the time or circumstances, and the value of this portion of Scripture to us is that Nehemiah shows us how to handle opposition successfully.

Latent in these opening chapters of the book of Nehemiah are the principles of a "task-specialist" and a "social-

emotional expert." Those who are interested in "role differentiation" within groups and wish to study "group dynamics"
will find that chapters 4 through 6 are freighted with practical
information.

The building of the wall—a task many believed to be
impossible—is completed in fifty-two days; and Nehemiah, having achieved his first objective, shows himself to be a wise administrator by immediately consolidating his gains (Nehemiah
7). His work is interrupted by a spiritual awakening which
takes place, for God sees that His people are unfit for self-
government and intervenes by bringing about a genuine
spiritual revival. During this time of renewal, Nehemiah wisely
takes a back seat. Ezra, together with the priests and Levites,
instructs the people in the Law. They keep the feast of tabernacles, and solemnly enter into a covenant with the Lord
(Nehemiah 8—10).

Only after the people are spiritually prepared for their new
responsibilities is Nehemiah able to continue with the work of
consolidation. This takes the form of repopulating Jerusalem
(Nehemiah 11), dedicating the walls of the city, and insuring
that the ministry of the Temple will be maintained (12:1—13:3).

The remaining years of Nehemiah's first term as governor
pass uneventfully. In 432 B.C., he returns to the Persian court
of Artaxerxes. He remains there for twelve years, and in 420
B.C. is again given the responsibility of governing the province
of Judah. When he arrives in Jerusalem, he finds that the people have departed from the Lord. He therefore engages in
vigorous reform and purges the people of the practices which
are depriving them of God's blessing (Nehemiah 13:5-31).

In our study of the book we will enlarge upon three important
topics: the basic characteristics of dynamic leadership; the importance of spiritual principles; and the necessity of sound administrative policies. As we work through these sections, we
will also examine Nehemiah's beliefs in order to determine the
contribution of his religious convictions to successful leadership. Our next chapter will give us some insights into what
made Nehemiah the great man he was.

1. What was Nehemiah's response to the news of Nehemiah 1:3? How did he reveal his concern? Consider the following qualities of leadership exhibited by Nehemiah (1:4): (a) his capacity to listen ("when I heard these words"); (b) his ability to identify himself with the needs of others ("I... wept and mourned"); and (c) his willingness to become involved ("I prayed before the God of heaven"). How may these three traits be used by you in situations you may be facing right now?

2. From a consideration of the Biblical teaching about Susa, what do you think were the particular problems Nehemiah might have faced as a man of God in such an environment (see Daniel 8:2; Ezra 4:9; Esther 1:2,5; 2:3,5,8; 3:15; 4:8,16; 8:14-15; 9:6,11,18)? Is there any similarity between the tensions he may have experienced and the difficulties you encounter?

3. Using your Bible dictionary or the maps at the back of your Bible, locate Susa. How long do you think it had taken Hanani and the others to journey to Susa from Jerusalem? Compare your estimate with Ezra 7:8-9. Ezra and those who were with him traveled with their wives and children. Note also Nehemiah 2:1-6 (Nisan is March/April) and 6:15 (Elul is August/September) for Nehemiah's own account of the time between making his request of the king and the finishing of the walls of the city.

Something to think about: As you continue your study of leadership, interact with the following statement by the renowned Jewish philosopher and historian, Dr. Mortimer Adler:

> The good leader must have *ethos*, *pathos*, and *logos*. The *ethos* is his moral character, the source of his ability to persuade. The *pathos* is his ability to touch feelings, to move people emotionally. The *logos* is his ability to give solid reasons for an action, to move people intellectually.

1

THE GREATEST FORCE ON EARTH

Nehemiah 1:4-11

Prayer has been called the greatest force on earth. There are some people, however, who feel that it is out of place in our highly sophisticated society. They tell us that with all our advancements in technology, prayer only impedes action. Others have even gone so far as to claim that belief in a vital relationship with God has been kept alive by the "puerile egos of inferior men."

In spite of these criticisms, there are many who have found that prayer has sustained them when the problems they faced seemed to overwhelm them. Abraham Lincoln admitted, "I have been driven many times to my knees by the overwhelming conviction that I had nowhere else to go. My own wisdom and that of those about me seemed insufficient for the day."

The Key to Excellence

In his "Memoirs" Nehemiah tells us of his experience with prayer. He came face to face with a situation which was too big for him. It concerned the people of God in "the province beyond the river." He was in Babylon and he felt powerless to help them. He turned to God in prayer; and from his example we learn how prayer may become an effective force in our lives.

As we take a closer look at Nehemiah we find that for prayer to be effective, it must be preceded by a knowledge of a need. Alan Redpath has pointed out, "Much of our praying is just asking God to bless some folks that are ill, and to keep us plugging along. But prayer is not merely prattle: it is warfare."[1]

[1] Alan Redpath, *Victorious Christian Service* (Westwood, N.J.: Revell, 1958), p. 23.

When Hanani and the others came to see Nehemiah, he asked them about the welfare of the people and the condition of the city of Jerusalem. To this general question he received a specific answer. "The remnant [lit., the left-over ones] are in great distress and reproach, and the wall of Jerusalem is broken down and its gates are burned with fire."

Jerusalem had been destroyed by the Babylonians in 586 B.C. (2 Kings 25:10). In spite of repeated attempts to rebuild the wall (Ezra 4:7-16), the city still lay in ruins. Without a wall to protect them, the people were defenseless. Robbers from the hills could come upon them unexpectedly and carry off their possessions. Because they were powerless to defend themselves, they lost status in the eyes of the other nations (see Nehemiah 2:17; 4:2-3; Psalm 79:4-9). Worse still, they lost their self-respect. They felt humiliated because, according to their own prophets, the walls of Jerusalem were to symbolize protection and her gates, praise (Isaiah 60:18).

A knowledge of the condition of his people moves Nehemiah to prayer. He weeps and mourns for them for days. He also fasts and prays to God on their behalf.

Some commentators believe that Artaxerxes was absent from the palace at the time Nehemiah received the news from Hanani. From chapter 2 it seems more likely that Nehemiah continued his duties and did not allow his personal concerns to interfere with his work. By comparing Nehemiah 1:4 and 2:1-2, we glean something of his self-control. He was quite unlike the Pharisees who wanted all men to see their supposed devotion (Matthew 23:14; Mark 12:40). Only after four months of intense prayer and self-denial did the king see any change in Nehemiah's general appearance.

Standing in the Breach [2]

In the verses which follow, we have preserved for us the kind of praying which produces results. We notice that for prayer to be effective it should also be conducted in an attitude of reverence.

[2] Psalm 106:23.

Nehemiah begins his prayer with adoration and worship. "I beseech Thee, O Yahweh,[3] God of heaven, the great and awesome God." His earnestness is obvious. He focuses his thoughts on the greatness of the One whom he is approaching. He stands in reverential awe of the majesty of God. He recognizes God's superiority as well as His sovereignty. The greater God becomes to him, the smaller becomes his problem.

Nehemiah's prayer is based upon Scripture.[4] He may have been reared in a land given over to idolatry and served in a pagan court, but this did not prevent him from cultivating his spiritual life (compare Colossians 2:6-7; 2 Peter 1:5-9). His prayer shows the extent to which he had mastered the Word and how it controlled his life.

In his prayer, Nehemiah includes praise. His thanksgiving is based on the character of God. He thanks God because He "keeps covenant and loving kindness with those who love Him and keep His commandments." The sons of Israel occupied a unique relationship to the Lord. After the custom of the ancient Near East, they were under an "overlord," or suzerain. In their case, their "Suzerain" was the "God of heaven." They were His subjects. He imposed His laws on them, and they were expected to obey His commands. In return for their loyalty, He gave them His protection. If they obeyed His covenant, they would enjoy His blessing (Jeremiah 11:4; 30:22; see Leviticus 26:12).

Nehemiah knew that the captivity had been brought about by the Israelites' breaking God's covenant. He nevertheless gives thanks that, in contrast to other rulers who would speedily punish offenders, their Suzerain is merciful (Psalm 103:8; 117:2; Joel 2:13), and preserves His loving-kindness with those who keep His commandments.

As Nehemiah continues his prayer he moves from worshipful adoration to entreaty. His attitude is one of earnest persistence based on the fact that God will respond to the need of His people if they will again submit to His authority (see 1 Kings

[3] The Hebrew word YHWH, Yahweh, is generally rendered LORD in most English versions. It differs from the other names of God in that it is used specifically of Him in His *covenant relationship* with Israel.

[4] Nehemiah's thinking must have been saturated with the Word of God for he quotes passages such as: Deuteronomy 4:25-31; 5:10; 7:9,21; 9:29; 30:1-5; Leviticus 26:27-45; 1 Kings 8:29; 2 Chronicles 6:20,36-40; 7:15; and Psalm 130:2.

8:29-30,52; 2 Chronicles 7:14). With this confidence he continues, "Let Thine ear now be attentive, and Thine eyes opened to hear the prayer of Thy servant which I am praying before Thee now, day and night, on behalf of the sons of Israel, Thy servants."

The prayer pattern which Nehemiah follows is most instructive. It parallels the "outline" the Lord Jesus gave to His disciples (Matthew 6:9-13; Luke 11:2-4).

There are many today who, when they pray, follow the same progression of thought which Nehemiah followed, but without his results. They begin with worship and move to entreaty. But they fail to persevere. Nehemiah's persistence is noteworthy. He continued in prayer for his people day and night. He might have done what we so often do, namely promise to pray about someone's need only to forget our commitment as soon as they pass out of our presence. Or he could have prayed for them once or twice and then left everything to the Lord. Nehemiah, however, persisted in prayer until God answered him. He did not regard prayer as the mere pushing of a button that would summon a bellhop. He did not think of God as a "cosmic bellboy" who would jump to do his bidding. He knew that when God takes a hand in our affairs, He uses means. In this instance, and at this time, prayer was the means God was using to accomplish His purpose (Ezekiel 36:37). Nehemiah did not expect God to answer his summons the moment he prayed. Instead, he recognized his subordination to his Sovereign and respectfully persisted until God answered him (James 5:16-18).

Not only does prayer aid in bringing our lives into conformity to the will of God, it also prepares us to receive the answer. As we become more conscious of God's purpose we frequently see the part we are to play in His plan. Persistent prayer then serves the purpose of strengthening our resolve. We receive new confidence. This confidence lifts us out of the realm of hopeless dejection and gives us the faith to persevere until we have achieved what God desires.

The attitude of Nehemiah's prayer is important. It stands in marked contrast to some prayers which fail to show respect for the One to whom the prayer is addressed. Nehemiah's attitude is one of reverence and submission. He knows that the self-sufficient do not pray, they merely talk to themselves. The self-satisfied will not pray; they have no knowledge of their need. The self-righteous cannot pray; they have no basis on which to approach God.

Removing All Barriers

By focusing his thoughts on *who* God is, Nehemiah becomes conscious of a barrier which is preventing their Suzerain from renewing the privileges of the covenant relationship. It is the unconfessed sin of the people. This illustrates another lesson in our prayer life, namely that for prayer to be effective, it must be accompanied by confession. Nehemiah knows that sin lies at the bottom of their present predicament. He therefore confesses, "We have sinned against Thee." Not wishing to blame the nation alone, he identifies himself with the guilt of his people: "I and my father's house have sinned." This confession would be particularly appropriate if Nehemiah was a descendant of the line of David.

Beginning with this general confession, Nehemiah then launches into specifics. "We have acted very corruptly against Thee, and have not kept the commandments, nor the statutes, nor the ordinances which Thou didst command Thy servant Moses." In saying this, Nehemiah obviously believes that the continued distress of Jerusalem is directly related to the unconfessed sin of the people. He also tacitly admits that the people have no merit of their own. They have broken their covenant with the Lord. He, however, has made provision for their restoration to His favor. And this provision becomes the basis of Nehemiah's petition.

In claiming the provision God has made for His people to be restored to His favor, Nehemiah shows another principle of prayer: for prayer to be effective it must be based upon the promises of God. "Remember Thy word," he says. Then, by paraphrasing the teaching of Deuteronomy 4:25-31; 30:1-5; Leviticus 26:27-45; and 2 Chronicles 6:36-39, he claims the fulfillment of God's promise. This appeal marks the high point of his prayer. His confidence in the Lord is so complete that he knows God will work out the details. He concludes by referring to the people as God's "servants." This implies renewed submission to His authority and the reestablishment of their former covenant relationship.

Nehemiah's intercession underscores the truth of Dr. R. C. Trench's observation that "prayer is not overcoming God's reluctance; it is laying hold of His highest willingness."

Nehemiah continues entreating the Lord's favor for four months (see Nehemiah 1:1 [November/December] and Nehemiah 2:1 [March/April, 445 B.C.]). During these weeks he comes to see the issues more clearly than ever before. He also begins to understand the part he is to play in the answer to his own prayer. All of this is evident from the way Nehemiah closes. He asks the Lord to prosper him as he makes his plan known to King Artaxerxes. He knows that it will be harder for him to leave the Persian court than it was for him to enter it. He is a trusted courtier and one whom the king relies on for his safety. Nehemiah does not know *how* God is going to work things out. His trust in the Lord is such that he confidently expects Him to take care of the details.

The Man God Uses

As we review this passage we find that it contains several important principles for today's leaders. One of these is that a leader must have a real concern for others. When Nehemiah received the delegation from Jerusalem, he showed an immediate interest in the welfare of the people and their city. When he learned of their plight, he became personally involved. He fasted and prayed for them.

All too often a would-be leader tries to climb the ladder of success by treading on others. He exploits their abilities to secure his own advancement. The importance of a vital regard for others has been stressed by Sir Arthur Bryant. In an article published in the *Illustrated London News*, this renowned historian said: "No one is fit to lead his fellows unless he holds their care and well-being to be his prime responsibility, his duty . . . his privilege."

A wise leader places the welfare of those with whom he works high on his own priority list. He insures that their concerns are taken care of ahead of his own. He knows that if they are relatively free from personal anxiety, they can perform better on the job. No business corporation or church, educational institution or mission, can succeed in achieving a goal without the willing assistance of those who are prepared to give of themselves for the sake of the work. The concern of an able administrator is shown in the way he treats his employees: his recognition of their contribution, and the manner in which he rewards their service (see Ephesians 6:9; Colossians 3:1).

This is not only sound policy for those who occupy the executive suites, it is practical counsel for aspiring businessmen, pastors, and mission leaders as well. A leader who closely identifies with those whom he leads will be able to motivate them to greater accomplishment. He will be able to estimate their individual capacities, weld them into a unit, and challenge them with personal and corporate goals. As Bernard L. Montgomery pointed out, "the beginning of leadership is a battle for the hearts and minds of men."[5]

This brings us to a second principle of successful leadership. While a vital concern for people is a necessary prerequisite to winning their confidence, and a close identification with them is the key to motivation, the importance of prayer should neither be ignored nor neglected. On a wall of one of the halls of Spurgeon's College, London, has been painted in large letters Christ's words: "WITHOUT ME YE CAN DO NOTHING" (John 15:5). By prayer we are able to enlist the power of God; for in prayer we ask God to do what we cannot do.

Unfortunately we tend to undervalue prayer. It is so secret and so silent that we often overlook it as if it were unimportant. The late J. Edgar Hoover spoke to correct this impression. He said, "The force of prayer is greater than any possible combination of man-controlled powers, because prayer is man's greatest means of tapping the infinite resources of God."

Nehemiah found prayer to be a great source of power. He was faced with a problem which was too big for him and he brought the whole matter to the Lord. God then showed him the solution. Through prayer Nehemiah was given a new *perspective* on the problem, he was led to reestablish his *priorities*, and he was given a sense of *purpose*.

As a result of Nehemiah's prayers for his people, a seemingly insurmountable problem was reduced to manageable size. At

[5]Viscount Montgomery, *The Path to Leadership* (London: Collins, 1961), p. 10.

the end of four months of intense intercession, God had given Nehemiah the solution to the problem.

Prayer also gives us a new *perspective*. The founder of the Penney Stores used to tell his colleagues, "True prayer opens the eyes to things not seen before. It stands in contrast to that prayer which has been the mere reflection of one's selfish desires." The greater God becomes to us, the better will be our perspective on our situation and the problems we face.

By becoming aware of what God wanted done, Nehemiah was led to reorder his *priorities*. He came to understand his role in the solving of the dilemma of his people. He found that he was to become a vital part of the means God would use to achieve the ends for which he had prayed.

We have no means of knowing how often prayers have changed the course of history. We do know that as a result of Nehemiah's prayer, God stepped into a seemingly hopeless situation and, working through one man, accomplished what seemed to be impossible.

Prayer not only established Nehemiah's priorities, it also gave him a sense of *purpose*. The realization that God had sent him would sustain him through the vicissitudes he would face as he began rebuilding the wall of the city. In what God accomplished through Nehemiah, there is encouragement for us. He is ready and willing and able to do the same through us if we will but learn the secret of unlocking His power. Our "groanings which cannot be uttered" are the prayers which God cannot refuse (Romans 8:26-27). Our daily prayers lessen our daily cares. They also keep us in the place where God can use us.

It is prevailing prayer that makes the difference! Exactly what kind of a difference, and how faith and works go together, is explained in our next section.

1. Read through Nehemiah 1:4-11 and make a list of the characteristics of prayer (e.g., earnestness, reverence, praise, etc.) that are suggested by Nehemiah's words and attitude. Which of these characteristics of prayer do you find the easiest to practice? Which are the most difficult?

2. Note the connection between Nehemiah's prayer and his inquiry into the situation of those in Jerusalem (1:2). This tells us a great deal about a competent leader. For example, he is knowledgeable of people's needs; he is personally concerned; he habitually brings before the Lord those whose needs are known to him; and he is willing to invest himself in others. Describe some of the things that happen when these principles are ignored. Why do you think people overlook these basic principles of sound leadership? How might you better emulate Nehemiah's example?

3. If you are meeting with a group, discuss ways in which you can present the essence of Nehemiah's prayer—i.e., his reverence for God, his recognition of the effects of sin, his respect for the covenant, and his resolve to act—to the people in a setting of your choice (e.g., church, a Sunday school, or a home Bible class). If you are studying on your own, put down your thoughts with the illustrations you would use.

Something to think about: In his book *The Essence of Prayer* E. M. Bounds said:

> Prayer has to do with the entire man. Prayer takes in . . . his whole being, mind, soul, body. It takes the whole of man to pray, and prayer affects the whole of man in its gracious results. As the whole nature of man enters into prayer, so also all that belongs to man is the beneficiary of prayer . . . . The men of olden times who wrought well in prayer, who brought the largest things to pass, who moved God to do great things, were those who were entirely given over to God in their praying.

2

THE DYNAMICS OF INTERPERSONAL RELATIONSHIPS

Nehemiah 2:1-8

Why do some middle managers succeed whereas others fail? What are the most common areas of weakness? How may pressures from above and tensions from beneath be turned to good advantage?

A young DCE of my acquaintance found herself caught in a typical middle management syndrome. Soon after graduating from college she was interviewed by the Christian Education Committee of a large church. "We are looking for someone who is innovative, 'on the ball,' and not afraid to make changes," they said. This description fitted my friend perfectly. She was offered (and accepted) the position as director of Christian education of this church. It wasn't long, however, before she found herself stalemated by her senior minister. She found it was *he* who ran the church, not the board; and *he* was opposed to change!

In such a situation, what could she do? How could she cope with a person who appeared to be so determined to block her every move?

In the same city there was an aspiring young manager. His skills were beyond question. In fact, the directors of his company had already marked him out for promotion. He was moved to a new department to gain experience. There, to his chagrin, he found his plans continuously thwarted by his immediate superior. Production schedules began to fall off, deadlines were not met, customers became irate, and he became frustrated.

In a very real sense these two people illustrate the somewhat facetious, but painfully obvious truth: middle management is like being caught between the proverbial rock and a hard place.

Middle management involves being able to translate the ideals of one's superiors into practice and, at the same time, knowing how to motivate one's subordinates. It necessitates keeping corporate goals in mind, while encouraging individuals to strive for personal achievement.

Nehemiah 2 describes the principles of successful middle management. From Nehemiah's example we learn the importance of loyalty and tact, how to avoid an unnecessary polarization, the technique of good questions, and the way the administration may be encouraged to adopt our ideas.

As our chapter opens, Nehemiah is waiting for his prayers to be answered. He knows that the king is the key to the solution of the problem, and he has prayed that Artaxerxes will be compassionate toward him (Nehemiah 1:11).

During a banquet at which Damaspia, Artaxerxes' queen, is present, Nehemiah takes up wine to give to the king. Perhaps their eyes do not meet as formerly, or perhaps something in Nehemiah's manner gives the king cause for concern. In any event, Artaxerxes notices a change in Nehemiah's attitude (Nehemiah 2:1b). He immediately suspects a plot against his life. "Why is your face sad [lit., bad], though you are not sick? This is nothing else but sorrow of heart!"

The predicament in which Nehemiah finds himself is unexpected. He has prayed for God's favor and blessing and instead he finds his loyalty to the king called in question.

The Middle Management Syndrome

Nehemiah immediately assures Artaxerxes of his loyalty. "Let the king live forever," he says. To be sure, this is a cliché. Kings before Artaxerxes had heard the same kind of sentiment from those who were plotting their assassination. However, since the words come from a man of Nehemiah's obvious sincerity, the king appears willing to believe him. He allows him to continue.

By assuring the king of his faithfulness to the crown, Nehemiah lays an important foundation for the explanation of his concern. Had Artaxerxes not believed his avowal of devotion, Nehemiah would have found it difficult to explain his "sorrow" of heart.

In replying to the king's question, Nehemiah says, "Why shouldn't my face be sad when the city, the place of my fathers' tombs, lies desolate and the gates are burned with fire?" This answer shows Nehemiah's tact. By replying with a question he avoids becoming defensive. If he had tried to justify himself (as we often attempt to do) he would only have made things worse. Then, the more he attempted to explain the cause of his sorrow, the less credible his story would sound. By answering the king as he did, Nehemiah avoided an unnecessary polarization and preserved the unity of their relationship.

A second illustration of Nehemiah's tact is found in the explanation of his grief. He is aware of the ancestral reverence which prevailed through the Near East. He therefore refers to the desecration of the graves of his forebears. He knows full well that this will arouse the sympathies of the king.

It should also be noted that at no time does Nehemiah mention the name of the city of his fathers. This is not deceit; it is the judicious avoidance of a potentially volatile subject. Jerusalem had gone down in history as a troublesome city (Ezra 4:6-16). Artaxerxes knows of Nehemiah's ethnic origin; and Nehemiah is wise enough not to prejudice his chances of success by stirring up unfavorable recollections in the mind of the king. Nehemiah's task is made doubly hard because he desires permission to return to Jerusalem and rebuild the wall—the specific thing which Artaxerxes had previously forbidden (Ezra 4:17-22).

Nehemiah's handling of this unexpected situation underscores the importance of tact. Tact does not mean that we have to agree with everything a person says. Nor does it mean that we have to lie to keep from hurting others. Tact is based on the truth *and* character, *and* an understanding of human nature. It involves knowing how to approach people, and how to make our requests known.

Clear Mandate

Nehemiah's discretion results in the king asking, in effect, "In what way can I help?" Nehemiah immediately sends off a "prayergram" to Heaven. He feels the need of extra help as he places before the king his plan and makes his requests known.

Christian businessmen, church leaders, and missionary statesmen frequently find themselves in the same kind of situation Nehemiah faced. They too need to ask the Lord for special help or direction before going in to a board meeting, presenting a controversial proposition to their employers, handling a trying customer, taking a potentially difficult telephone call, or entering into delicate negotiations with a manufacturer or supplier (see Psalm 50:15; 91:15; Isaiah 65:24).

In answer to the king's general question Nehemiah responds with specifics. "If it please the king, and if your servant has found favor before you, send me to Judah, to the city of my fathers' tombs, that I may rebuild it. . . . Let letters be given me to the governors of the provinces beyond the river, that they may allow me to pass through . . . and a letter to Asaph the keeper of the king's forest, that he may give me timber." As Alan Redpath has pointed out in *Victorious Christian Service*, Nehemiah wanted to know that he had been *sent*, that he would be kept *safe* while away from the palace, and that he would have his needs *supplied*. His reply reveals how well he had done his homework. He knew exactly what he needed.

Nehemiah's opening statement contains an important principle for those in middle management. We will not get far with our new ideas if we do not involve our bosses in what we have to suggest. By prefacing his request with his statement, "If it please the king . . ." Nehemiah preserved Artaxerxes' superiority. The king did not feel threatened. Nehemiah was inviting him to make the decision. He was suggesting that the crown take the initiative. His whole attitude showed Artaxerxes that he was loyal to him.

Nehemiah's courteous opening paves the way for his requests. These are established upon the basis of the king's confidence in him. They grow out of Nehemiah's loyalty and willing submission to the king's authority. Once again, no mention is made of the name of the city, nor is there any reference to the king's previous decision (Ezra 4:21), which must, of necessity, be amended. All Artaxerxes asks is, "For how long will your journey be, and when will you return?" And Nehemiah gives him a definite time—twelve years (Nehemiah 2:6; 5:14; 13:6).

Allowing Nehemiah to go to Judah will mean great personal loss to Artaxerxes. This has caused some writers to conclude that there must be an error in the text, for Artaxerxes, they reason, would certainly not allow such a valuable employee to be gone from court for so long a period of time.

In answering this question, it should be pointed out that there had been trouble in Syria only two years before. The satrap (or viceroy), Megabyzus, had headed a revolt against Artaxerxes. Megabyzus, however, had been forced into submission and although Artaxerxes distrusted him, for political reasons, he retained him in office. It suited Artaxerxes' purpose to have someone of Nehemiah's loyalty separating Syria from Egypt. With Nehemiah in Jerusalem, alliances between these countries will be more difficult to form.

But how are we to explain Nehemiah's success? What may we learn from his example?

Nehemiah's success in presenting his petition to the king may be attributed to the fact that he prepared himself ahead of time. Had he not done so the conversation might have ended with his commission to go to Judah, but without the other things he needed. Without the necessary preparation in Babylon he would not have had the necessary materials for the task in Judah. A few months earlier, when he realized that God intended him to be a part of the answer to his own prayers, he began anticipating his needs. As he assessed the situation, he knew of only one person who had the resources he needed to rebuild the city—Artaxerxes. He was also cognizant of the obstacles that might prevent the successful completion of his assignment. He knew that before he could begin rebuilding the city, he must have safe passage through the different provinces. He was aware of the dislike of the different satraps for the Jews, and knew that they and their subordinate officials might interrupt his journey and hinder his work unless he had authoritative credentials to present to them. Only the king's seal would do!

Having done his "homework" well, Nehemiah is aware of his

needs. He therefore lists his requests. "If it please the king, let letters be given me for the governors [of the provinces] beyond the river, that they may allow me to pass through until I come to Judah" (Nehemiah 2:7). Obtaining this kind of authorization from Artaxerxes is good business policy. It shows proper foresight. These credentials would place his work squarely under the aegis of the king.

It is surprising how frequently this kind of provision is either overlooked or ignored by people in business and church circles today. A few weeks ago I lunched with a man who had recently joined the staff of a Southern California library. His immediate supervisor had served the university for fifteen years. With expansion, the administration found that the supervisor could no longer handle his department. They decided that as soon as a new specialist could be found, they would perform what Laurence Peter calls "a *lateral arabesque*—a pseudo-promotion consisting of a new title and new work place."

The problem was that the administration never clarified their new appointee's role with the other employees. As a consequence, he found himself in a position of responsibility, but without the necessary authority. The administration expected him to take over from where his former boss left off, but the employees under him did not know that he was the new department head. With such a poorly defined role, the other department heads would not cooperate with him.

When I talked with this librarian, he was seriously considering an appointment elsewhere. All of this could have been avoided if the administration had given him what Nehemiah requested, namely authority commensurate with his responsibility, and the public clarification of his place on the administrative chart.

Secondly, Nehemiah asks for his needs to be supplied in a way that will be worthy of the one who is sending him to Judah. "Let another letter be given me to Asaph, the keeper of the king's forest, that he may supply me with timber to make beams for the gates of the fortress which is by the house [of God], and for the wall of the city, and for the house into which I will enter."

Interestingly, Nehemiah knows of the close proximity of one of Artaxerxes' forests (lit., "paradise") to Jerusalem, and the name of the man in charge. He has also learned of the layout of the city from Hanani.

Having done so much to prepare himself for this interview with the king, we might expect that Nehemiah would congratulate himself on his success. Instead, he writes, "and the king granted all these things to me because the good hand of my God was on me." His dependence on the Lord is real. His humility is genuine. And his example reminds us not to boast of the things God does through us as if we had accomplished them unaided.

The Impossible Dream

God works in human affairs to accomplish His purpose. What had begun four months earlier as an impossibility was now beginning to appear possible. And the key? Prayer, preparation, and perseverence.

Prayer is a deliberate identification with God and His purpose. Christians everywhere bear testimony to the efficacy of prayer. Charles Trumbull stated: "Prayer is releasing the energies of God. For prayer is asking God to do what we cannot do." And Nehemiah was a man of prayer.

Nehemiah was also an astute student of human nature. He prepared himself well. He was familiar with the king's plans and ambitions, problems and anxieties. His sensitivity to Artaxerxes helped him as he laid his plans before the king. His approach highlights the importance of loyalty and tact, the need for advance preparation, the importance of avoiding any unnecessary polarization, and the best way of preserving a superior's autonomy.

A knowledge of human nature will also lead us to be cautious. We cannot trust everyone we meet. Jealousy and rivalry are all about us. When we take on a new assignment we should ask for the public clarification of our role so that others will not hinder us from carrying out the mandate given to us.

Finally, there is perseverence. Nehemiah did not stop after the king had granted his initial request. He continued with his petition until all his needs had been supplied.

The problems of middle management can be handled easily and effectively if we will study the personalities of those about

us. Absorption with technicalities is a poor substitute for knowing how to get along with people. Promotions, in most cases,
come because of a subordinate's sympathetic understanding of
his superior's problems. Those who have studied the
characteristics of the people with whom they work—on a
tridimensional level: above, on a par with, and below
themselves—will be more useful to their employers and more
successful as well!

THE PSYCHOLOGY OF GOOD QUESTIONS

Good questions help to clarify situations as well as dispel
doubt and suspicion. Nehemiah used questions to good advantage. His question to Artaxerxes not only provided a rationale for his downcast appearance, it caused his superior to
reflect on the condition of those in one part of his realm. It
made him aware of the plight of the Jews. Nehemiah was then
able to follow up this advantage and, without alienating his
employer, lead to the answer to his prayers.

The Lord Jesus used questions throughout His ministry. He
used questions to begin a conversation (John 5:6). He reasoned
with questions (Matthew 12:24-30). He taught with questions
(Matthew 18:12). After telling the crowd the story of the good
Samaritan, He asked, "Which of the people in the story do you
think proved to be a neighbor to the man who fell into the hands
of the robbers?" (Luke 10:36) On another occasion when the
religious leaders tried to trap Him with their hostile, in-
criminating query, the Lord Jesus rebuked them with a question (Luke 22:48; Matthew 22:17-21). A great deal of His
recorded ministry was conducted by means of questions. He
used questions to hold His listeners' attention and also to
stimulate their thought processes.

Questions can be used to handle almost any situation.
However, they should not be employed so as to hold others up
to ridicule. If our attitude is one of kindness we will be less likely to antagonize others. We must insure that our questions are
not used as a cloak for our own anger. If we betray angry feelings we will immediately place the other person on the defensive. It is preferable to ask, "Could we discuss this together?"
or, "Do you feel this is the right course of action?" By using

questions such as these we will be able to approach a difficult situation in an objective way.

Sometimes it is difficult to think of a good question on the spur of the moment. This is why we need to become familiar with human nature. The better we know the characteristics of the person with whom we are dealing, the more easily will we be able to ask the right questions.

One of the most difficult situations to handle is a potentially hostile person. We never know when our motives will be misunderstood or our intentions maligned. I once worked for a company whose president was given to violent outbursts. His secretary was the only one who could handle him. I set myself to learn how she did it. I found that she would ask him a "what" question, not a "why" question. "What's upsetting you, Mr. Brown?" Then she would let him talk. This had the effect of being cathartic. Mr. Brown would discuss his latest annoyance, ventilate his feelings, and obtain a better perspective on the situation.

It is also difficult to handle an argumentative person. Sometimes these people appear to be very sincere. However, if we sense that our answer will lead to a debate, it is better to ask for a clarification of the issues. This can easily be done. "Why do you ask?" we might say; or, "What is your opinion?" If they counter by saying, "But I want to know what you think," we can then reply, "I'll be happy to share my thoughts on the subject with you as soon as I know why you are asking the question."

We will find that the more skillful we become in the use of questions, the more readily will our questions accomplish their purpose. Sometimes they will stimulate thought. At other times, they will tactfully expose folly. They may also reveal another's motives and intentions. And on occasion, they may even challenge or direct.

Frequently the real issue is not the substance of the situation, *but how the other person feels.* A well-worded question can restore confidence and maintain open communication without loss of face.

Fitting the right question to a given situation is an art. Questions can be used to good effect wherever we are, whether at church or in the office, at home or while visiting friends. The secret lies in our development of a few basic skills. These skills are exemplified in Nehemiah.

In summary, a "why" question (such as the one Artaxerxes asked) presupposes authority, probes for a convincing rationale for one's behavior or decision, and generally places the person addressed on the defensive. A "what" question, on the other hand, generally asks for an opinion and necessitates that the individual questioned think through the issues and provide a logical answer.

1. In considering the situation of Nehemiah, we find that he exhibited the characteristics of a faithful subordinate: (a) he had the patience to wait, and while he waited he prayed (compare Nehemiah 1:1 with 2:1); (b) he had the courage to act (2:5); and (c) he possessed the ability to persuade (2:6b-8). In assessing these virtues, what can you learn from Nehemiah that will help you in some of the practical aspects of your present work?

2. What is the value of a person's being in touch with his feelings? Nehemiah was candid about his emotions (Nehemiah 2:1-2,8).

    Nehemiah was also in touch with the feelings of others—hence his tact. How was this tact demonstrated? What were probably Artaxerxes' chief concerns?

    How did Nehemiah, through his sensitivity to the feelings of the king, allay his sovereign's anxieties and open the door for the acceptance of his proposal?

3. As we "read between the lines" we learn something of the extent of Nehemiah's planning before he made his request to the king. Make a list of his plans including the specifics. Why is planning ahead hard for some managers? What are some of the results of the failure to plan ahead?

4. Some managers have difficulty delegating authority to their subordinates. What might have happened had Nehemiah not asked for authority commensurate with his responsibilities? How did he guard against being caught in a situation where others might effectively challenge his authority or where the job to be done might exceed his resources? In what practical ways might these principles of delegation be applied by you in your work?

Something to think about: Nehemiah, the "number two" man in the winter palace of King Artaxerxes, is commissioned to go to Judah and undertake a task many believed to be impossible.

Consider the words of E. F. Girard as they apply to Nehemiah and to yourself:

> Leadership is achieved by ability, alertness, experience; by willingness to accept responsibility; by a knack for getting along with people; by an open mind and a head that stays clear under stress.

3

TAKING COMMAND

Nehemiah 2:9-20

Some years ago a new branch manager was appointed to the company I worked for. He was to replace a very popular man whose unique abilities had early marked him out for promotion. It was a difficult situation for the new man. He knew that a favorable reaction to his appointment was essential. He also felt the need to assert his authority.

In making his plans this new manager wisely arrived in town two weeks before he was due to assume his responsibilities. He kept himself in the background and studied the situation thoroughly. Then, on his first day in office, he scheduled a meeting of all department heads. At the meeting he began by praising the men. He complimented each one on his individual achievement. Then, with a deliberate change in his attitude, he continued: "But I don't care what you've done in the past! From now on...."

The result of this assertiveness is not hard to imagine. Morale took a nose dive. Discontent prevailed. Instead of a smooth transition, the new manager created barriers that would take months to overcome.

All of this causes us to ask, Is there a right way to take over a new position of leadership? Are there any proven techniques that will help us surmount these hurdles?

The dynamics involved in situations like this are illustrated in Nehemiah 2. These dynamics include both *internal* and *external* forces.

Nehemiah had formerly been a cupbearer. In this position he had been, in a sense, under the eye of his sovereign. Now, as governor, he was far removed from any direct supervision. He was on his own. And he was facing the kind of situation in which many men fail. The strategy which he employed as he took over his new assignment contains important principles for us today. It can be applied to any external situation we are called upon to face. As we shall see, his strategy involved challenging, motivating, and encouraging those in Jerusalem.

After discussing the external forces Nehemiah faced as he assumed the governorship of Judah, we will then turn our attention to the *internal* dynamics which might have affected his leadership.

Envoy of the King

During Nehemiah's journey from Susa to Jerusalem, he was accompanied by a band of soldiers (Nehemiah 2:9). They ensured his protection and added to his prestige as he presented the royal credentials to the border officials. In all probability, he journeyed from Susa to Babylon and then took the shortest route through Tadmore to Damascus—a journey of about two months. The Oxford historian, George Rawlinson, conjectures that, from Damascus, Nehemiah followed the Jordan valley to the ford opposite Jericho and then took the main road to Jerusalem.[1]

The enemies of the Jews in Samaria soon learned of Nehemiah's arrival. We read that "when Sanballat the Horonite and Tobiah the Ammonite official heard about it, it was very displeasing to them that someone had come to seek the welfare of the sons of Israel."

But how did Nehemiah learn of their displeasure?

It is true that, based on the experiences of the Jews in the past (see Ezra 4:4-24), Nehemiah probably anticipated opposition. Yet, this does not account for his intimate knowledge of the reaction of those in Samaria (see Nehemiah 4:1-3,7-8,15-16; 6:1-2; etc.). The only possible explanation is that Nehemiah sent to Samaria personnel who would keep him informed of any activities contemplated or planned by the enemies of the Jews. If this is so, then it shows his realism (see Matthew 10:16). He was not naive. He didn't trust those who already had a history

[1] George Rawlinson, *Ezra and Nehemiah: Their Lives and Times* (London: Nisbet, 1890), p. 94.

of opposing the welfare of those in Judah. He trusted the Lord implicitly and took adequate precautions as well. His example shows us how faith and works operate together.

Opposition to Nehemiah centers in Sanballat, the governor of the province of Samaria. He is called "the Horonite" and was probably from one of the Beth-Horons ("house of [the god] Horon," see Joshua 16:3,5), and a descendant of the mixed group that settled in Samaria after the Assyrian conquest (2 Kings 17:24,29-31). His associate is an Ammonite named Tobiah (see Deuteronomy 23:3). Tobiah is from an old and famous family who have ruled Ammon for generations.[2] In verse 19, the name of Geshem is added to the list. He is a powerful Emir who has recently united the Arabs into a vast confederacy and whose Bedouin armies dominate the eastern and southern area of the Dead Sea.

Paradox and Promise

Nehemiah's arrival in Jerusalem undoubtedly disturbs the power structure of the city. From what we later learn of the priests and the rulers (see Nehemiah 5:5,7-10; 6:7-19; 13:4-9), we may be sure that they viewed his coming with concern. All Nehemiah records is: "So I came to Jerusalem and was there three days." We may well inquire, What did he do during those three days?

Some writers believe that the "three days" were occupied with ceremonial purification. This is possible. From verses 12b and 16, however, it seems likely that Nehemiah also looked the situation over and obtained firsthand information—information which Hanani could not have given him. Furthermore, in the light of Nehemiah 3, it seems probable that during these three days he was planning his strategy for building the wall, assessing the leadership of the people, calculating the needed resources, and providing for effective channels of communication. Possibly he was also waiting for the right psychological moment to make his plans known to the people.

[2] This fact is attested by the Zeno Papyri and by palace and tomb remains found at "Araq el Emir" in Jordan.

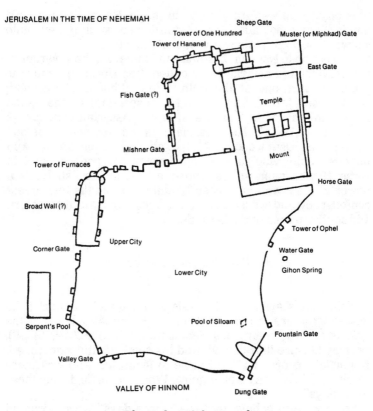

JERUSALEM IN THE TIME OF NEHEMIAH

The Pulse of the People

At the end of the three days, Nehemiah's activities have
aroused considerable interest (Nehemiah 2:16). Even his delay
in making his plans known is working to his advantage. He is
aware of the importance of waiting for the right moment to tell
the people the purpose of his visit and wisely keeps his counsel
to himself until he is ready to act.

Only when Nehemiah is in possession of all the facts, does he
convene a meeting of *all* the people. He makes sure that
everyone has the opportunity of seeing him in person and hearing firsthand what he has to say. No one is given the responsibility of interpreting his remarks to others.

While the text does not say so, it is possible that the lumber for the scaffolding either had arrived or was on its way. Nehemiah was wise enough to know that if he is to challenge the people to rebuild the wall, he must be prepared to set them to work at once. A delay would only dissipate their enthusiasm and give his enemies time to counteract his moves.

As Nehemiah addresses the people, he calls on them to evaluate their situation. "You see the bad situation *we* are in." They had lived with their present circumstances for so long they had become apathetic. It was necessary for them to be reawakened to see their real need. Nehemiah begins by focusing their attention on the problem. He also links himself with them by using the pronoun "we." This prepares them for the challenge. "Come," he says, "let us rebuild the wall of Jerusalem that *we* may no longer be a reproach." This arouses their patriotism. It also shows Nehemiah's close identification with them. They begin to realize that Nehemiah is not like other governors (see Nehemiah 5:14-18). Instead of seeking his own personal ends, he is interested in them. His genuine concern for them gives them confidence in his leadership.

Some years ago a young man was appointed to the position of assistant pastor of a midwestern church. When he met with the board he was specifically asked to upgrade the Christian education department of the church. Within two weeks of his appointment he had alienated his teachers. His abrasive manner did not pave the way for cooperative relationships. His criticism of the teaching methods of the Sunday school staff, and scornful "*I* want all *my* teachers to take a refresher course to improve their skills" caused many to resist his ideas.

If this youthful assistant had begun his work by assessing the situation, calculating the mood of the Sunday school, and treating the teachers as equals, he might still be with the church. As it happened, his stay was mercifully short.

Setting Goals

Nehemiah is a wise leader. He knows that the objective he sets for the people must be attainable. If he aims too high and they are unable to reach the goal he sets, they will become

discouraged and lose confidence in him. And so to his challenge
he adds encouragement. He tells them "how the good hand of
his God has been favorable to him." He explains all that
transpired in Babylon and how the Lord had not only opened
the way for him to come to Judah, but had also provided the
materials for the repairing of the wall. He also shares with
them news of the king's decree (Ezra 4:17-22). By pointing them
away from their fears to the Lord he fixes their minds on what
God is doing for them. This reassurance is of great encouragement to the Jews. They realize afresh that God is on their side.
Their enthusiasm is ignited. They immediately respond: "Let us
arise and build!"

Nehemiah's handling of the situation in Jerusalem illustrates
for us the essence of good motivation. The significance of what
he accomplished may be seen from the fact that for ninety
years the people had been saying, "It can't be done!" Now they
are united and eager to begin the work of rebuilding the
defenses of their city.

This new zeal would quickly have dissipated if Nehemiah
had not been able to put them to work. It is probable that
Nehemiah had matters so well in hand that the people could
begin rebuilding the wall of the city without delay. So enthusiastic are they, that Nehemiah is able to conclude this section of his "Memoirs" by saying, "So they put their hands to the
good work."

The Formidable Alliance

As with all work for the Lord, when once a person or a group
begins to do something for God's glory, opposition is only a
stone's throw away. News of what Nehemiah is doing travels
quickly. When Sanballat the Horonite, Tobiah the Ammonite official, and Geshem the Arab, hear of it, they mock the Jews and
despise them, saying: "What is this thing that you are doing?
Are you rebelling against the king?"

An insinuation that the Jews were rebelling against Artaxerxes had previously been sufficient to cause the work to
cease (Ezra 4:13). Those in Samaria try the same strategy
again, knowing full well that weak, demoralized people are inclined to give way before threats. But they reckon without

Nehemiah! Before the Jews can react, Nehemiah makes his reply (Nehemiah 2:20). His answer is firm and dignified. In the eyes of the men of Samaria the Jews may appear to be weak and unequal to the task. Their confidence, however, is not in themselves but in the Lord. With this assurance, the mockery and insults of their opponents are unable to affect them. Nehemiah's next statement places everything in a totally new perspective. "But you," he says, "have no portion, right, or memorial in Jerusalem." This is something they had not expected. And the men who had come to disrupt the work return to those who sent them inwardly disturbed and bearing disconcerting news.

It should be pointed out that, in his reply, Nehemiah shows both his courage and his discretion. He boldly confronts those who are attempting to thwart what he is doing and, at the same time, avoids being drawn into a debate. He refuses to argue. He states the reason for his confidence: "the God of heaven will give us success." By emphasizing the spiritual nature of their task, he brings a new dimension into what they are doing. This takes the responsibility for success out of the hands of the Jews. As long as Jerusalem is a reproach to the Jewish people, it is also a reproach to their God. Inasmuch as this work is God's work, His servants will arise and build the city.

It is not too difficult to imagine the admiration of the Jewish people for Nehemiah. In this one encounter he has successfully routed their worst enemies.

Behind the Manager's Desk

We all, at one time or another, change jobs or pastorates, or are given a promotion. When this happens, *external* and *internal* dynamics begin to operate. The way in which Nehemiah handled himself as he took over his new responsibilities, challenged, motivated, and encouraged the people, and dealt with opposition, contains important principles for us. He illustrates how we may handle the external forces we all face. With some, however, promotion goes to their heads. They become harsh and authoritarian in their attitude. Others, on the other hand, become afraid of offending or alienating those with whom they work. And some find that they cannot get along without peer approval.

Nehemiah sets men, in this kind of situation, a much needed example. As far as the external dynamics are concerned, Nehemiah *checked things out* in order that his decisions might be based on facts. *He aroused the interest of the people* and wisely withheld details regarding his plan and purpose until he was ready to act. He then *convened a public meeting* and gave everyone the opportunity of hearing him in person and of interacting with his ideas. He *challenged* them with the work to be done, *motivated* them to undertake the task, and *encouraged* them with assurance of success.

It is also probable that Nehemiah expected a crisis. He was not naive enough to think that his ideas would please everyone. If this is so, then he knew that sooner rather than later, he could expect opposition from those in Samaria.

These factors, however, are all external, and success is based as much on inner strength as on outward strategy. Of primary importance, therefore, is the way Nehemiah handled inner conflicts.

The problem of inner conflicts is twofold. First, the person appointed to a new position of responsibility needs to realize that these conflicts are internal; secondly, he needs to insure that his actions are grounded in reality. If they are not, he will find himself constantly making and then undoing decisions. The result will be confusion—to himself and to his subordinates.

Many managers and church leaders tend to place these internal conflicts outside of themselves. A person who finds himself unable to operate efficiently is likely to look for an explanation in the external setting in which he operates. He may blame the administration or the church board for his failure, or excuse himself by claiming that inadequate authority has been delegated to him. He may also blame incompetent or inadequate help for his inability to meet deadlines or prepare his messages. In reality his problem may be internal. His failure may be the result of anxiety over *status* (his new position as a leader and his responsibility for production, etc.), or anxiety over *competition* (feelings of inferiority).

Anxiety over status comes when a young person is promoted

and finds that he loses his former popularity. This loss of popularity affects him in different ways. His former supervisors now regard him as a competitor. His former peers must now respond to his supervision. If the new leader's internal dynamics are such that he must have acceptance, then he experiences anxiety over his new role and may attempt to minimize his new position and play down his authority. If this happens he is headed for trouble.

As we evaluate Nehemiah's change of roles, we find that the favorite of Artaxerxes' court left the security of the palace for the trials and hardships of governing a downtrodden people. Nehemiah, however, did not confuse or try to obliterate the change which had taken place in his responsibilities. He did not become a "people-pleaser" for the sake of popularity. Neither did he diminish the status of his office in order to win acclaim. He knew only too well that those who play up their likability or strip their office of the symbols of authority, sooner or later shred the respect of their colleagues. They neutralize their effectiveness and inadvertently provide their employees with a negative image of the rewards of achievement.

By far the commonest expression of anxiety, however, comes from fear. Those who have recently been elevated to positions of managerial responsibility fear retaliation if they assert their authority. They also fear the opposition of those who hold positions of responsibility on a level with theirs. Sometimes this is caused when one is called upon to take a stand on a controversial issue. The weak leader will tend to vacillate, talk out of both sides of his mouth, and resort to hyperactivity in order to avoid facing difficult problems.

Here again, Nehemiah sets us an example. He avoided the fear-syndrome[3] because his confidence was in his God. He believed his steps were ordered of the Lord (Psalm 37:23) and that He would not allow anything to befall him which was not ultimately for his good (compare Romans 8:28). This confidence strengthened him as he took over his new responsibilities, commenced the task of rebuilding the wall of the city, and faced the opposition of his enemies.

Anxiety over status is, however, only one of the problems facing Christians who assume positions of responsibility. The

[3] The whole concept of fear will be discussed in chapter 8.

second is in the area of *competition.* In combating this feeling it
is absolutely essential that the new pastor or manager have a
keen sense of reality, including spiritual as well as corporeal
truths. It must prepare him for give-and-take in making decisions and in solving problems. Whereas this characteristic will
be further elaborated on in our consideration of Nehemiah 4
and 5, the basic principles of how to face opposition are found
in this section.

As we further analyze the situation, we find that those in
positions of responsibility experience anxiety over competition
or opposition for two main reasons: fear of failure and fear of
success.

Fear of failure generally stems from a feeling of inferiority.
The individual feels that he lacks ability. As a result he fails to
have a strong identity. In this connection it is of value for us to
notice that when Nehemiah took office his confidence in the
Lord assured him of success. To borrow the words of the
Apostle Paul, Nehemiah was "bold in his God to do the work
without fear" (1 Thessalonians 2:2). He knew that fear of
failure could be resolved only by drawing his identity (i.e., his
personal strength) from the Lord. He therefore established a
basis for reality in the unchangeable God. This done, he was
able to adjust to the problems which faced him.

But what of the *fear of success?* Success is not wrong. It is
the inordinate desire for advancement which leads eventually
to failure. In *Macbeth,* Shakespeare uses Scotland's king to
show us the fear which "success" produces. In the case of
Macbeth, it was guilt over his misdeeds that led him to suspect
that others were plotting against him. The specter of his
assassination of the former king haunted him. As a result,
there were very few whom he trusted. His strongest subordinates were most suspect and his administration centered in
those who were the least qualified to lead others.

When Nehemiah took office he knew that it was a result of
divine appointment (see Psalm 75:6-7). He did not feel that his
"success" was at the expense of anyone else. As a consequence he was not plagued by guilt feelings, and his sense of
reality was not distorted. Later on, as we shall see in chapter
11 (Nehemiah 7), he appointed as leaders people who were the
most capable he could find. He did not, as Macbeth, elevate to

positions of responsibility those from the ranks who would not threaten his position.

Because Nehemiah had a strong identity, he could take up the reins of administration in Jerusalem without trying to impress people with his "nice-guy" qualities. He was not plagued by either the fear of failure or the fear of success. His leadership was always from a position of strength. This strength was derived from spiritual forces which had been developed through the years. With such internal dynamics at work within him, and pervading all he did, it is not surprising that he could face a seemingly insurmountable task, motivate a downtrodden people, and handle opposition—all with equanimity and apparent ease.

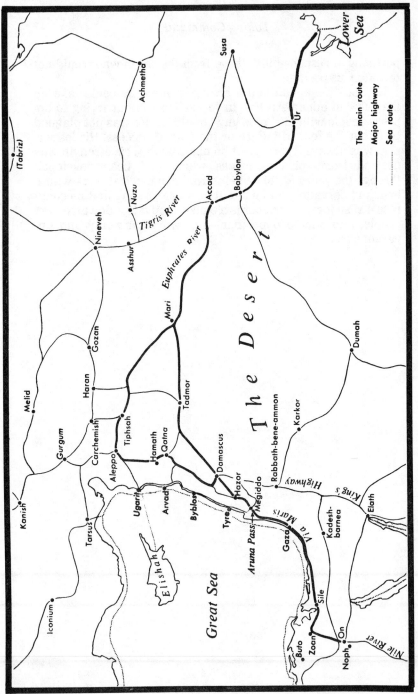

MAJOR HIGHWAYS AND TRADE ROUTES OF THE ANCIENT NEAR EAST

1. In considering Nehemiah 2:9-16, put yourself in Nehemiah's position. What would you have had turning over in your mind between Nisan (March/April) and Tammuz (June/July) while you were en route to Jerusalem? How would you have anticipated sharing your goals with those in Jerusalem? Would you have prepared for opposition (all the way from indifference on the one hand to open hostility on the other)? How? Why?

2. Nehemiah knew human nature. From a consideration of what we are told of Sanballat in Nehemiah 2:10,19; 4:1-2,7; 6:1-2, 4-7, 12-14; 13:28, what kind of person do you think he was? What can be gleaned from his attitudes, words, and actions? How would you have handled him?

    Tobiah, too, is prominent in the record. Consider what the Bible tells us about him, his relation to Sanballat, and what his words reveal about his personality (see Nehemiah 2:10,19; 4:3,7; 6:1,12,14,17,19; 7:62; 13:4,7,8). In what ways was he different from Sanballat? What is the best way of dealing with such a person?

    Geshem (Gashmu) completes the trio. Consider how Scripture speaks of him in Nehemiah 2:19; 6:1-2,6. What kind of opposition did Nehemiah face from Geshem? Describe his counterpart in contemporary society.

3. By using the chart on page 40, trace Nehemiah's nocturnal inspection of the walls of the city. Why had he not told the leaders in Jerusalem of his plans? As far as Nehemiah was concerned, what factors may have combined to make the "right" time for him to reveal what "God was putting into his mind to do for Jerusalem" (Nehemiah 2:12)? Timing is important in leadership. How would you have gauged the right time, or as some call it, the "psychological moment," if you were Nehemiah?

4. In motivating people, many companies provide incentives—extrinsic rewards (i.e., an extra bonus, an all-expenses-paid vacation to Hawaii, etc.)—without realizing that the effects

of such incentives are marginal; these incentives must be repeated again and again, and increased, in order to make employees strive for them. How did Nehemiah motivate those in Jerusalem? How did he create in the people of Jerusalem a desire to be different? In what ways did Nehemiah take a positive, personal approach to the problem? What incentives did Nehemiah give the people?

Nehemiah's attitude was infectious. The people of Jerusalem caught his optimism. How did Nehemiah capitalize on their new enthusiasm?

Something to think about: Interact with the following statement by J. Sterling Livingston that appeared in the *Harvard Business Review*:

The way managers treat their subordinates is subtly influenced by what they expect of them. If a manager's expectations are high, productivity is likely to be excellent. If his expectations are low, productivity is likely to be poor.

4

FORMULA FOR SUCCESS

Nehemiah 3

It is interesting to read different people's formulas for success. Some emphasize the need for hard work whereas others stress the importance of integrity. One individual will philosophize about interpersonal relations while another will theorize about problem solving, the setting of goals, or on-the-job training of employees. Seldom can agreement be found on all that is involved.

In view of the prevailing uncertainty, it is well for us to observe that God has illustrated the basic principles of success in Nehemiah 3. The chapter is easy to analyze. Each paragraph is structured around one of the gates of the city. The message of the chapter, however, is not as easily learned. Many writers have attempted to draw spiritual lessons from the real (or imagined) significance of the gates. Others have concentrated on the names of the people. All will agree that Hebrew names are significant. Unfortunately we do not know enough about the meaning of the names or the character of the people who bore them to determine if their names have any special significance. In view of the prevailing uncertainty most modern commentators confine their remarks to the physicial features of the city. Others ignore the chapter altogether.

The problem we face as we look at this chapter—at the long list of names—is that we are tempted to turn the page and continue the story at Nehemiah 4. Yet this chapter is one of the most important in the entire book! By noting repetitious statements, certain vitally important principles emerge. From these principles we will learn the secret of Nehemiah's success.

To Each His Own

The first principle of success is seen in the *coordination* Nehemiah achieved. The clue is found in the recurrence of the phrases "next to him" or "next to them" (Nehemiah 3:2ff) repeated throughout the chapter. During the three days Nehemiah was in Jerusalem, he must have planned his strategy well. He knew where each person or group would work, and he assigned the men from Tekoa, Gibeon, Jericho, and Mizpah, etc., to sections of the wall where no residents were close at hand.

The very fact that these phrases occur so often yields still another truth. Each person knew where he belonged. He also knew where his responsibility lay and what was expected of him. Some workers had the responsibility of rebuilding their section of the wall from scratch, while others needed only to make repairs. Regardless of whether they were involved in building or repairing, each person knew what his job entailed. In all their work, there was coordination of effort.

A second set of recurring phrases enlarges upon our understanding of this principle of coordination. It is found in the words "over against his house" or "beside his house" etc. (Nehemiah 3:21-23,28-30) In assessing the importance of this we find that Nehemiah took advantage of convenience. He did not have people "commuting" from one end of Jerusalem to the other.[1] This would have wasted time and reduced efficiency. It would also have made it difficult for the workers to be fed. Furthermore, in the event of an attack[2] by their enemies, each man's concern would have been for his family. If his family were somewhere else in Jerusalem, he would have no way of protecting them. By arranging for each man to work close to his own home, Nehemiah made it easy for them to get to work, to be sustained while on the job, and to safeguard those who were nearest and dearest to them. This relieved each worker of any unnecessary anxiety. It also insured that each person would put his best effort into what he was doing.

---

[1] The only "commuters" were those who lived outside the city (see Nehemiah 4:12).

[2] Nehemiah 4—6 deals with a series of crises which arose while the rebuilding of the walls was in progress.

B. C. Forbes was quite right when he spelled *success* "t-e-a-m-w-o-r-k." His observation that "if the whole prospers [the individual worker] as an active, effective, progressive part of it, will prosper with it" deserves continued emphasis.

Few people can appreciate the importance of coordination until they have encountered the kind of chaos which exists without it. A friend of mine accepted the position of district superintendent of his denomination. In recent years everything had been going wrong. Giving to missions had dwindled, numbers had eroded, and some churches had even closed their doors. It wasn't long before he found that there was an almost total lack of communication between the head office and the churches. There was also a corresponding failure on the part of the pastors to cooperate with each other. He had to begin by regulating and harmonizing the efforts of all involved. This was not an easy task, but once it was achieved, the results were quite dramatic. His experience proved that there can be no lasting advance without proper coordination.

This principle holds true in business and industry, church and hospital, home and school. In his autobiography, Bernard L. Montgomery tells of his experiences when he took over the leadership of the Eighth Army in North Africa during World War II. He found the men demoralized and lacking cohesion. His first task was to enthuse them with his own dynamic and then to coordinate their activities. The result of his strategy is well known. It turned the tide of the war.

The basis of all effective leadership is the proper coordination of the activities of all involved.

Pulling Together

The second principle of success in leadership is found in the *cooperation* Nehemiah achieved. Men from different places and different walks of life worked together on the wall. These included priests and Levites, rulers and common people, gatekeepers and guards, farmers and "union men"— goldsmiths, pharmacists, merchants—temple servants and women.

The priests might have absolved themselves of responsibility for working on the wall by pleading their special consecration to sacred things. It is to their credit that they took the lead in the rebuilding program (Nehemiah 3:1ff)! Likewise, the goldsmiths might have excused themselves. After all, they were used to intricate, delicate work, not the clumsy, cumbersome task of laying bricks. Their willingness to cooperate with the others is truly commendable.

It is also interesting to notice that certain bachelors cooperated in the rebuilding of the wall,[3] even though they did not have wives and children to protect (Nehemiah 3:23). There were also the rulers from the two districts of Jerusalem who willingly left their comfortable quarters to labor shoulder to shoulder with the laboring classes. They worked without rivalry or resentment. In making his rounds, Nehemiah could not help but notice that one of the officials, a man named Shallum, was being assisted by his daughters. This fact is both interesting and important. Women were rarely mentioned in the Near East and when their activities are recorded in the Bible, it indicates something very significant. These young women showed that they were not afraid to do work normally assigned to men.

Then there were the men from Jericho, Tekoa, Gibeon and Mizpah, Zenoah and Beth-Haccherem, Beth-Zur and Zelah. They had very little to gain by fortifying Jerusalem, and could easily have allowed their own concerns to draw them away from such profitless work.

There were also different kinds of "union men." They belonged to the guilds. If their guilds were the same as our unions today, these men would have had to cross picket lines because Nehemiah was not paying union wages.

Unfortunately, it has become fashionable in our day for employees to do as little as possible for as much as possible. This was not the old New England philosophy, which held that work in itself was rewarding, even necessary, for the full enjoyment of life. There are some students of our American society who believe that America became a great nation because its people believed that if the job was worth doing, it was worth

---

[3] Meshullam, the son of Berechiah, carried out repairs "in front of his cell"—a small one-room dwelling. He was not a bachelor, for Nehemiah 6:18 indicates he had a daughter of marriageable age. He probably lived outside Jerusalem and left his wife in their home when business took him to the city.

doing well; that a man's diligence, his pride in performance, and his dedication to work were all qualities of character greatly to be admired. We need a return to this kind of outlook and to the ideals which gave rise to it.

Furthermore, people in charitable organizations and leaders in our churches frequently lament the quality and quantity of work done by volunteers. Nehemiah, however, had the ability to motivate people, not only to give of their time, but also to give of their best. And these people—all of them—worked willingly because they had a mind to work (Nehemiah 4:6)!

It is important for us to know that Nehemiah did not achieve total success. The elite from Tekoa would not support the work in Jerusalem and refused to participate (Nehemiah 3:5). Nehemiah, however, did not allow their obstinacy to deflate his optimism. He worked with those who were willing to put their backs to the work of the Lord, and succeeded in accomplishing what many believed to be impossible.

Nehemiah's volunteers set an important example. They were coordinated in their activities. All concerned worked together to rebuild the wall. In addition, the cooperation Nehemiah achieved shows the extent to which he was able to weld together this diversified group. Everyone had a common objective.

The Vital Dimension

A third principle of Nehemiah's success may be found in *commendation* he paid the workers. What he did is of particular significance to us today.

We are living in an era of depersonalization. The companies from whom we buy merchandise are far more interested in our driver's license and credit rating than in insuring the quality and reliability of *their* product! To the Internal Revenue Service we are merely a number, and to the Census Bureau, a statistic. This causes us to lose our identity. We begin to doubt our worth and, after a while, realize that if, for some reason, we failed to show up for work or dropped dead, few would miss us.

In this chapter, Nehemiah tacitly shows us the need to take a personal interest in our employees. This is evidenced by his knowledge of the names of those who worked on the wall, and his awareness of where they worked and what they did. He treated them as people, not as things. They had worth and were not there to be exploited.

Each one of us needs to feel that he counts for something. If we recognize this need in dealing with others, and show our appreciation in our attitude, we will have much better rapport with them. Commending people for their honest effort is one of the most valuable keys to successful human relations.

Nehemiah used commendation to enrich the quality of the lives of his workers. He was closely identified with them and available to encourage them when the going was rough. He knew that the work men do is an essential part of their lives. This is true, not merely because by means of their work they earn their bread (Nehemiah's workers were volunteers), but because a man's job gives him stature in the community and binds him to society. Nehemiah knew that the worker who is happy in his job, with confidence in the management and cooperative relations with his colleagues, will spread his contentment throughout the group.

Nehemiah's awareness of the effort of others is noteworthy. It is found in the recurring expression "repaired another section" (Nehemiah 3:11,19-21,24-27,30). He was quick to notice and appreciate the zeal and effort of those who worked with him. Of particular significance was the effort of the men from Tekoa (3:5,27). Their leaders opposed what Nehemiah was doing. The people of Tekoa, however, were inspired by his example. They worked diligently on repairing the wall. When their first assignment was finished, they repaired another section. They were more than statistics to Nehemiah. They were individuals—each with a life of his own—and they were important to him for who they were, not only for what they did.

The recognition a leader pays his subordinates creates a sense of belonging. They feel secure. And this feeling of security is absolutely essential when difficulties arise or economic pressures make their presence felt (see Nehemiah 4—6).

In pursuing the thought of commendation, we would have expected Nehemiah to praise Hanun and the inhabitants of Zanoah, for they repaired fifteen hundred feet of broken-down wall (Nehemiah 3:13). But right next to them was Malchiah

who, working alone, only repaired the Refuse Gate (3:14).
Nehemiah commended Malchiah's honest effort as well. He did
not allow the size of one person's accomplishments to prevent
him from recognizing the efforts of another.

In thinking about Nehemiah's commendation of his workers,
we may well ask, Where did *he* work? What did *he* do? This
Nehemiah does not mention. He is not numbered among those
who must forever be pushing themselves forward to achieve
praise from others. He knew that in a well-managed enterprise
a good leader always takes a little more than his share of the
blame and a lot less of his share of the credit. He was happy to
give others a place in the spotlight, and wisely kept himself in
the background.

Finished Business

Another principle of success may be seen in the fact that
each person *completed* the task assigned to him. The words
"built" and "repaired" are in the perfect tense. Each one kept
busy. Each one knew what was expected of him. Each one
worked in his place. And each one finished the work he had
undertaken.

This all sounds too simple: coordination . . . cooperation . . .
commendation . . . completion. It is! But there is one further
dimension: *communication*. It involved the instruction of each
worker so that he knew what to do and where to do it, and the
delegation of authority so that decisions did not have to be constantly referred back to the top.

Richard J. Wytmar, writing in *Automotion* magazine, pointed
out that "one of the most universal traits of leadership and success is simplicity. This is the capacity to cut the problems down
to size; to explain even the most complex of situations in the
simplest of terms. It is the art of using words, gestures, and
behavior that are simple, common, and understandable to all
people, and therefore, easily communicable."

Nehemiah coordinated his activities by dividing the wall into
about forty different groups. Each person was assigned a section on the wall. By breaking the work up into sections,
Nehemiah was able to supervise the work and communicate
with one section at a time. What was formerly a complex situa-

tion, became relatively simple when handled piecemeal. From chapter 2:17-20, we know that Nehemiah was able to speak to people in simple, understandable terms. His instruction of the different classes of people (with their varied experience) on how to build the walls, must have been as easy to comprehend.

Added to this was the delegation of authority. Each person was able to assume responsibility for his section of the wall. Groups of workers had section heads (e.g., Hanun was "*over the inhabitants of Zanoah*" [Nehemiah 3:13]; "*the Levites carried out repairs under Rehum*" [3:17]; etc.), and power to make decisions was delegated to the leaders of each group. If this had not been Nehemiah's practice he would have become bogged down with petty decisions and could never have coordinated the activities of all the groups.

In the final analysis, Nehemiah succeeded because he was employee-centered and followed the important basic principles of effective leadership. He *coordinated* the efforts of the workers, insured the *cooperation* of the different groups, *commended* honest effort, saw that each task was satisfactorily *completed*, and provided for adequate *communication*.

These principles of effective leadership may be applied to whatever the Lord has given us to do. They apply equally as well to politics and commerce as they do to education and missions, private enterprise and industry. By following Nehemiah's formula for success, we too, may lay the foundation for our own leadership.

THE PSYCHOLOGY OF EFFECTIVE LEADERSHIP

Society places a high premium on individuals who have the ability to lead others. More and more effort is being spent on "executive search" and "management development" today than ever before. Key positions are continuously opening in commerce and industry, government and civil service—all to the right man with the mystical "something."

But where are leaders to be found? Or, a little more to the point, What are we looking for in someone who is to lead others?

Years ago, psychologists spent considerable time and money evaluating the personal qualifications of leaders. The characteristics tabulated by these teams were little more than arbitrary, and the lack of consensus led to confusion. Emphasis on the personality of the leader dealt with only one aspect of the problem. What of the situation itself—the people the leader worked with, the pressures he faced, and the problems he had to overcome?

It wasn't long before the personality of the follower was considered alongside the personality of the leader. This in turn highlighted the importance of effective human relations.

Writing in *Banking* magazine, William T. Hocking and Robert M. Wald pointed out that "the successful top executive . . . will have to be trained as a professional in human dynamics and leadership, whether he reaches the top position through general management or through a specialty. He will also have to be an effective short-and-long-range planner—and an implementor of plans."

Maintaining effective interpersonal relationships was one of Nehemiah's strong points. The extent of his personal ability may be gauged from the number of the groups and the diverse kinds of the people he welded into a unit. Not only did he keep them working, he kept them working harmoniously in spite of their differences in social status, geographic origin, and professional occupation.

Modern researchers, in pursuing their studies of leaders and their problems, have finally begun to focus attention on the different kinds of leadership responsibilities. Two main characteristics emerged: the task specialist, and the social-emotional expert.

The *task specialist* organizes the group, sets a goal, and directs their activities toward the achieving of this objective. The *social-emotional expert* maintains group morale, preserves harmony, and often works toward relieving tension between employees.

The task specialist, so the researchers found, was emotionally more distant from the individual members of the group than the social-emotional expert. He often did well in a wide variety of situations which required organizing skill and the ability to maintain emotional distance. Social-emotional leaders, on the other hand, also did well in many different settings, particularly where effective functioning depended upon constructive personal relationships. Ideally these functions should be carried out by the same person, but not every leader has the ability to play both roles.

Nehemiah was able to function both as a task specialist and a social-emotional expert. In Nehemiah 2:17-20, we see him setting a goal and then motivating those in Jerusalem to work together to achieve it. He is very much the task specialist, and all his organizing skill is geared toward achieving his objective. In chapter 3, Nehemiah is seen in a dual role. He is intimately connected with the workers and assures that they are able to function effectively. In chapter 5, we shall see him as the social-emotional expert becoming involved in the problems of those working on the wall and working out a satisfactory solution.

After the wall has been built and the work of consolidation begins, Nehemiah will set new and different objectives and become more of an administrator.

The abiding point is that many men in the upper echelons of business and industry frequently fail because they cannot change roles as Nehemiah did. The man who began a company five years ago, built it up from nothing, and is now its president and chairman of the board, may find that he can no longer hold things together. He blames his misfortunes on "unforeseen economic trends" and excuses his inefficiency because "you cannot get reliable staff these days." The truth of the matter is, the company needs a different kind of leadership. The founder functioned well as a task specialist but is a failure as a social-emotional expert.

Nehemiah knew himself; he knew people. He had developed the ability to change from one role to another and, as a result, succeeded where others often fail.

TIME FOR REFLECTION

1. What would you consider to be a good formula for success? Having read about Nehemiah, how would you define successful leadership? What qualities or characteristics would you include in your ideal leader?

2. What does the Bible teach about Nehemiah's strategy as he faced a seemingly impossible task? To discover how he analyzed the need and then implemented a plan of action, outline Nehemiah 3. Give each paragraph a title in keeping with some significant work done (e.g., 3:1-2, "Rebuilding the Sheep Gate," etc.). According to this outline, how did Nehemiah divide up the work?

3. How often does the term "next to him" or "after him" occur in Nehemiah 3? What do you think God is trying to teach us about the principles of successful management through this repetition?

4. Three primary styles of leadership have been labeled (1) authoritarian, (2) authoritative, and (3) permissive. Using today's terminology, what style of leadership do you think Nehemiah followed? In what ways did he allow for freedom of choice (see Nehemiah 2:18; 3:1,5b,20,27,30)?

5. What evidence can you derive from Nehemiah's example of efficient ways to delegate responsibility? How does this evidence support your view of his leadership style?

   In light of Nehemiah's example, why do you think people need to be commended for their efforts? What is generally an employee's response to deserved praise?

   How may an employee's response be changed by the manager's leadership style (authoritarian, authoritative, permissive)? What evidence is there in Nehemiah 3 to support the view that "positive reinforcement" led some of those who were building the wall of Jerusalem not only to give of their best, but to do more than their allotted share of the work?

Something to think about: When interviewed by *Nation's Business*, Walter Finke, chairman of the board, Dictaphone Corporation, said:

> My theory of a business is that the top and center core be as small as possible and that the maximum possible authority be given to the people running the individual ventures making up the enterprise. I believe in pushing down responsibility and authority so that we get more good younger people into the organization and they have an opportunity to advance and, hopefully, share the rewards.

5

A COMMON DILEMMA

Nehemiah 4:1-6

Some years ago, A. J. Murphy propounded his famous *law.* He said, "If there is any chance of something going wrong, you can be sure it will."[1]

In secular business, and in our work for the Lord, things "go wrong" for internal or external reasons. We are either inadequate for the job and fail to plan as we should, or outside forces arise which we cannot control. The way we cope with these problems reveals the caliber of our leadership.

In our evaluation of the way Nehemiah built the wall of Jerusalem, we find that he took on a task he had never tackled before. From an "internal" point of view, he did all that could be expected of him. He prepared for his new responsibilities, he knew what was expected of him, and he made adequate provision for his needs. If we had only the information contained in chapter 3 as our guide, we might conclude that, as a result of his organizational ability, the work on the wall went ahead without any mishap. Opposition, however, arose from a quarter Nehemiah could not control. The way in which Nehemiah handled these "external" pressures is most instructive.

In analyzing the relationship of Nehemiah 3 with chapters 4, 5, and 6, we observe that in chapter 3 Nehemiah tells us *what* happened—the Jews built the wall. Chapters 4—6 tell us *how* it was done—in the face of severe opposition. Significantly, the kind of opposition Nehemiah faced is the same kind we face today. In Nehemiah's response we learn how we too may effectively handle external threats.

[1] Quoted in Lester R. Brittel, *Management by Exception* (New York: McGraw-Hill, 1964), p.65.

OPPOSITION TO THE WORK OF THE LORD

Opposition from Without	Opposition from Within	Opposition from Without
4	5	6
Nature of the Opposition		
1. RIDICULE _Recourse:_ Prayer 2. THREAT OF VIOLENCE _Recourse:_ Prayer and Watchfulness 3. DISCOURAGEMENT _Recourse:_ Reorganization and Workers Armed	GREED AND OPPRESSION _Recourse:_ Open Confrontation, Restitution, and Prayer	1. INTRIGUE _Recourse:_ Manly Firmness & Prayer 2. INNUENDO _Recourse:_ Open Denial & Prayer 3. INTIMIDATION _Recourse:_ Exemplary Conduct and Prayer

The Human Predicament

In the opening verses of this chapter, we have another indication of the way in which Nehemiah kept himself informed of all that took place in Samaria. It is reported to him that as soon as Sanballat hears that the wall is being rebuilt, he becomes furious. In his anger he mocks the Jews.[2] "What are these feeble Jews doing? Are they going to restore [the walls] for themselves? Can they offer sacrifices? Can they finish in a day? Can they revive the stones from the dusty rubble—even the burned ones?" (Nehemiah 4:2)

But why is it necessary for Sanballat to speak to the powerful political forces of Samaria in this way? What adequate cause is there to explain his violent outburst?

Put bluntly, "a powerful Jerusalem means a depressed Samaria." One of the main highways linking the Tigris-Euphrates river valley to the north with Egypt in the south and Philistia to the west, passes through Jerusalem. With Jerusalem once more a well-protected city, its very location will attract

[2] Sanballat ridicules the Jews before the "army of Samaria"—the local militia made up of the influential men of the city and the residents of the province.

trade; and gone will be Samaria's economic supremacy in "the land beyond the river."

In mocking the Jews, Sanballat unconsciously follows a pattern of opposition which has been employed through the ages. He begins with contempt. "What are these feeble Jews doing?" he asks rhetorically. Through his disdain he attempts to lower their self-esteem, weaken their resolve, and destroy their morale.

We have all met people such as Sanballat. They take delight in putting others down. They will pass the office of someone who has recently received a promotion, or been given an important assignment, and say: "You don't really believe all that the boss said about you, do you?" Or, "They've only given you the job while they look around for someone else." Their scornful words immediately put us on the defensive and take the joy out of what we are doing. As with Sanballat, they aim at discouraging us so that we will not be able to give of our best.

Sanballat continues his attack by maligning the Jews' motives. "Are they going to restore it [i.e., the walls of the city] *for themselves?*" In saying this he implies that they are selfish and have an ulterior motive. His immediate thought is, "What are they getting out of it?" The altruism of a person such as Nehemiah does not fit into any of his preconceived patterns of behavior. His attitude is the common response of worldly-minded people. They cannot understand how a person can do things for God's glory alone. In the same way that Sanballat mistook the motives of the Jews, so unbelievers today make the mistake of judging Christians by the standards they set for themselves.

The failure of a worldly individual to understand the work of the Lord is further shown by Sanballat's next questions. "Can they offer sacrifices?[3] Can they finish in a day? Can they revive

---

[3] Most writers believe that Sanballat here refers to the offering of sacrifices at the beginning of the work. This view is supported by ancient pagan literature and has as its basis the thought that if suitable sacrifices are made, the deities thus invoked will help the builders and prosper their efforts. Nehemiah, however, had begun the work on the wall. It was almost finished to half its height. It seems more likely, therefore, that Sanballat here refers to the offering of sacrifices at the completion of the building program. This ties in with his next question, "Can they finish in a day?" implying that their "feebleness" will hinder them from carrying out their resolve.

the stones from the heaps of dust—even the burnt ones which have crumbled to dust?" In this he implies that the job is too big for them, and that they will never be able to complete the project and dedicate the walls. They had tried before and had met with failure. What guarantee do they now have that they will be successful?

The impossibility of the task is depicted by the state of the materials. When the city was sacked and burned by the Babylonians, the fire caused most of the limestone walls to crumble. Their neglect of almost a century would have further rendered them useless for building. And so by describing the insuperable obstacles that lie in the way of the Jews, Sanballat presumes they will be unable to finish the task. But he fails to reckon with a group of people inspired by a leader who is himself motivated by God.

Following Sanballat's sarcastic outburst, it is Tobiah's turn to deride the Jews. "Even what they are building—if a fox would jump on it, he would break down." His imagery is most suggestive. Foxes are not only fleet of foot, but lithe and agile as well. A wall would have to be poorly constructed to be toppled over by a fox! It is the vividness of Tobiah's remark that has led some commentators to the conclusion that between verses two and three, Sanballat and the men of Samaria actually came to Jerusalem and watched the Jews at work.

Whether these words were spoken in the hearing of those working on the wall or came to their attention through intentional "leaks," they have the desired effect. The builders become demoralized. They have been subservient to those in Samaria for so long that hope dies quickly in their hearts.

How will Nehemiah handle this new development? What can he do successfully to counteract this malicious slander?

The Basis of Confidence

It is most instructive for us to notice that Nehemiah first brings the whole matter before the Lord (Nehemiah 4:4). A rebuttal would have led to heated words. By resorting to prayer, Nehemiah is able to give full expression to his feelings. He does not suppress his emotions or bottle up his anger inside him. Had he done so, it would have begun to warp his personality, distort his sense of reality, and destroy his relationship with the Lord.

Those who suppress their feelings generally do so because they have an idea—an external idea—of what Christian conduct should be like. This is sometimes diametrically opposed to the way they feel. By becoming concerned over what others will think of them they suppress their resentment and, as a consequence, become bitter and resentful.

Instead of suppressing his feelings, Nehemiah had recourse to prayer. Judging from the way he was able to inspire the Jews to continue with the work, his prayer, while personal, was probably public.

Prayer has many beneficial effects. Not only does it enable us to ventilate our feelings, it also gives us the opportunity to discuss matters with God and obtain a new perspective on our problems. If we would only pray over our difficulties, we would find that our anger or resentment would be dissipated. If we took time to tell the Lord about the things that disturb us, we would not be tempted to gossip to others about them. Prayer is a most important part of proper mental health. As the famous physician, Alexis Carrel, observed, "I have seen men, after all other therapy has failed, lifted out of disease and melancholy by the serene effort of prayer."

By praying over his problem, Nehemiah is led to recognize afresh that God is the omnipotent One. The rebuilding of the wall is His project. Recognition of this takes the whole burden of responsibility off Nehemiah's shoulders.

Word and Spirit

The exact nature of Nehemiah's prayer has long been a source of embarrassment to Christians. "Return their reproach on their own heads and give them up for plunder in a land of captivity," he prays. "Do not forgive their iniquity and let not their sin be blotted out from before Thee" (Nehemiah 4:5).[4]

But how are we to explain such a harsh and apparently vindictive prayer? It is so unlike the teaching of the Lord Jesus

---

[4] This is an example of an imprecatory prayer—the invoking of evil on another.

(Matthew 6:9-13; Luke 11:2-4), that God surely cannot expect us to use it as a model.

Some writers have tried to rationalize their way out of the problem by resorting to the original text. They claim that the verbs are predictive instead of imperative. This explanation, however, fails to stand up under closer examination. In the first instance, the context is against such an interpretation; and secondly, when Old Testament imprecations are repeated in the New Testament, the usage made of them shows them to be maledictions.

A second attempt to explain these imprecations tries to exonerate God from any part in the prayer. Those who hold this view take refuge behind the fact that the inspiration of the Scriptures guarantees only the accurate recording of what was said and does not necessarily imply divine approval. As far as the theory of inspiration is concerned, this is true. David, however, was a "man after God's own heart" and his writings are full of imprecations (see Psalm 5:10; 10:15; 28:4; 31:17-18; 40:14-15; etc.).

Realizing the flimsiness of these views, most commentators resort to another explanation. They point out that people living in Near Eastern lands were highly excitable and quick to invoke the curse of a deity on someone they disliked.[5] Once this point has been conceded, they go on to explain that these people knew nothing of grace; that the teaching about "loving your enemies" and "praying for those who persecute you" (Matthew 5:44-45) had to wait for the coming of Christ (see Luke 6:36; Ephesians 5:1). But such a view ignores the fact that grace is found throughout the Old Testament and was taught by Moses (Exodus 23:4-5; Leviticus 19:18), David (Psalm 25:12ff; 109:4-5), and Solomon (Proverbs 25:21-22).

Quite obviously there must be a better answer for imprecatory prayers than those which have been suggested thus far.

On one occasion, some seminary students asked a well-known Old Testament theologian how he explained the imprecatory Psalms. His answer was most revealing: "You have

---

[5] Examples of imprecations may be found in J. B. Pritchard's *Ancient Near Eastern Texts* (Princeton: Princeton University Press, 1959); and D. J. Wiseman's *The Vassal Treaties of Esarhaddon* (London: British School of Archaeology in Iraq, 1958).

to be a very spiritual person to pray that kind of prayer!" In applying this to the context of Nehemiah's prayer, we find that Sanballat and Tobiah, in deprecating the work, were in fact holding up to scorn and ridicule the God of the Jews. As the renowned Semitic scholar, C. F. Keil, has pointed out, "[They] openly challenged the wrath of God, by despising Him before the builders."[6]

The encouragement we derive from this comes from the fact that God takes personal note of what happens to us. Those who oppose us are, in reality, demonstrating their opposition to Him. This should serve to encourage us and show us how precious we are in His sight.

In praying as he does, Nehemiah shows how closely he is identified with the Lord and His work. Then he keeps the builders busy. While actively engaged in doing the work they have less time to worry about the slander of their enemies. This is not the time to sit down and discuss some new strategy. Prayer has restored his perspective. He knows the danger of delay. He is astute enough to realize that when their enemies see that their strategy has failed, they will resort to more drastic measures to stop the work.

So successfully does Nehemiah counter the evil influence of Sanballat and Tobiah, that he can write in his *diary*, "so we built the wall, and the whole was joined together to half its height."

But how were those workers who had become despondent (Nehemiah 4:5) encouraged to continue building the wall? What caused their dismay to change to determination? Why was Nehemiah later able to say of them that "they had a mind to work"?

The only satisfactory answer to these questions lies in the personality of the leader. As Bernard L. Montgomery so wisely pointed out, "A leader must have an infectious optimism, and the determination to persevere in the face of difficulties. He must radiate confidence, relying on moral and spiritual principles and resources to work out rightly even when he himself is not too certain of the material outcome."[7]

[6] C. F. Keil, *The Books of Ezra, Nehemiah, and Esther* (Grand Rapids: Eerdmans, n.d.), p.201.
[7] *The Path to Leadership*, p.11.

The Search Within

There is an attitude abroad today, particularly among evangelicals, that if we live right nothing can or will go wrong. This frame of mind is contrary to the Scriptures (Matthew 18:7; John 16:33). On one occasion the Lord Jesus told His disciples to take a boat and cross to the other side of the lake of Galilee. They obeyed and encountered a terrific storm (Mark 4:35-41). On another occasion the Apostle Paul saw in a vision a man from Macedonia beckoning him to cross over into Europe and help them (Acts 16:9-10). He did so and met with severe opposition (2 Corinthians 7:5). Trials and difficulties come our way even when we are in the center of God's will. The genius of Christianity lies in the fact that God enables us to overcome these difficulties while accomplishing the work He has assigned to us.

The secret of overcoming opposition lies in our relationship with the Lord. He has the ability to help us surmount the problems we face. Our emotions frequently control our outlook. Negative feelings destroy our confidence. They can be successfully counteracted only by faith. Our worrying over a situation will not make it go away. Anxiety never robs tomorrow of its sorrow, it only saps today of its strength. What we need when the doors of despair appear to be closing around us is faith—faith that expresses itself in prayer. Earnest, effective prayer will restore our perspective and replace our negative emotions with positive responses. This positive outlook will inspire hope; hope will give us renewed confidence; and the result will be an upsurge in morale.

From Nehemiah's example we also learn the importance of perseverance in handling opposition. Perseverance is the test of real leadership ability. It is one thing to set a goal or an objective for a group of people; it is quite another to persevere toward it and inspire others so that they are motivated to follow us.

Nehemiah's perseverance was established firmly upon the conviction that what he was doing was what God wanted done. As a result, he was able to rise above ridicule, counteract despair, and infect others with his own optimism. They received encouragement from his indomitable spirit. Instead of aimlessly licking their wounds, his example challenged them aggressively to tackle their problems. As they worked they found that their faith became stronger. They made progress. Whereas in their discouragement they had seen their troubles as mountains; now, with quickened insight, their difficulties appeared as clouds which were soon to vanish away.

From these few verses we learn to expect opposition, even when we are doing God's will; to develop positive responses to opposition through prayer and our identification with God and His purpose; and to persevere with the task at hand. Faith is always the vital ingredient. It led Nehemiah through the valley of despair and translated his efforts into noble achievements. His faith gave him confidence. His confidence inspired others. The secret of his success can become ours. As the Apostle John pointed out, "this is the victory that overcomes the world—even our faith" (1 John 5:4).

TIME FOR REFLECTION

1. The first form of opposition is ridicule. Why does Sanballat find it necessary to reassert his authority in the presence of, and also exert his control over, those in Samaria (Nehemiah 4:1-2)? What were his feelings? Why did Sanballat resort to ridicule? What did Sanballat hope to achieve by his actions (a) in Samaria, (b) in Jerusalem? Was Sanballat successful (4:5b)? Why do people today engage in ridicule? What do they hope to achieve?

2. The people in Jerusalem were dismayed by the ridicule of those in Samaria. Why are people vulnerable when they or the work they are doing is being criticized? In what ways does our denigration by others undermine our confidence (even as the caustic comments of Sanballat and Tobiah undermined the confidence of those in Jerusalem; compare Nehemiah 2:19-20)? Why do we then tend to become discouraged?

3. Nehemiah found his people demoralized. How long do you think it took before he became aware of what had happened? How did Nehemiah interpret what had happened? What key words in Nehemiah 4:4 describe the effect of Sanballat's slander on those in Jerusalem? If the people became discouraged because they did not keep their eyes on the Lord, what do we learn about the dynamics of effective leadership from (a) Nehemiah's example, (b) Nehemiah's prayer?

4. In Nehemiah 2:17-18 Nehemiah is seen motivating those in Jerusalem to undertake a seemingly impossible task. In 4:6 the results of his handling of opposition are apparent. How would you encourage a dispirited group of people (either in your church or your place of business)? Of what value is a clear spiritual perspective? How would you describe the impact of a strong personal Godward relationship on a group such as the one Nehemiah worked with in Jerusalem? How do you think Nehemiah's enemies in Jerusalem reacted to a drop in morale? What is the effect of strong leadership (as

seen in prompt action) on (a) those who are discouraged, and (b) those who would like to see the leader fail?

Something to think about: Nehemiah faced opposition without vacillating. He felt secure, even when others were trying to "unseat" or unsettle him. Joe Batten in *Tough-Minded Management* wrote:

> Security is about 20 per cent financial and 80 per cent emotional.... Personal earnings is *not* the answer to today's search for security. Self-confidence, self-knowledge, and an awareness of what you stand for will do much to insure [personal security].

6

VALUES IN CONFLICT

Nehemiah 4:7-23

Some years ago I came across these lines by an unknown author: "In times of adversity, many people lose their courage and display a weakness that is unnecessary. They assume that a loss, or a disappointment, is a failure when actually misfortune can mean opportunity." This same author went on to point out that "we must weave from our circumstances . . . the pattern and texture of life. Strength is gained by overcoming adversity, not by giving in to it."

From our experience we know this to be true. We should expect pressure. Learning how to handle it without losing our emotional balance, however, takes time. It involves growing toward maturity.

In the passage before us we find that Nehemiah is expecting Sanballat to take further measures to stop the building of the wall. He, therefore, spurs the workers on. The wall is completed to half its height for "the people have a mind to work." Morale is high. Unfortunately, under renewed pressure, the enthusiasm of the people begins to wane. Despair settles in. They become depressed and conclude that the fortification of the city can go no further.

We, too, face situations when those working under us feel that too much is being asked of them. There are times in the life of every pastor when he feels that adverse economic pressures or some opposition in the church makes it difficult for him to continue. As with Nehemiah, he feels the loneliness of his position. Those in commerce and industry know that the threat of cutbacks and layoffs destroy morale. Because external pressures and internal forces are situations all leaders face, we have a great deal to learn from the way in which Nehemiah handled the circumstances which confronted him.

Dilatory Tactics

When the enemies of the Jews find that their ridicule and threats have failed to stop the workers, they turn to violence. They completely surround those in Jerusalem. There is Sanballat to the north, Tobiah and the Ammonites to the east, the Arabs to the south, and the Ashdodites (the ancient Philistines) to the west. The leaders of these groups adopt a new strategy. They plan to intimidate the Jews by causing them to lose confidence in their leader.[1]

The root cause of the conspiracy is anger. Anger generally results from the *frustration* of one's plans, the *humiliation* he feels when he fails, or the hurt of *rejection*. The anger of Sanballat and his coconspirators is not hard to trace. They feel *frustrated* because their earlier strategy has failed (Nehemiah 4:1-6). This failure causes them to feel *humiliated* in the eyes of the influential men of the province. They had ridiculed the Jews for their feebleness and now find that they have been thwarted by them. As a consequence, they suffer from lowered self-esteem. They sense that the wealthy merchants and land owners now doubt their ability to deal with those in Judah. This causes feelings of *rejection*. The result is anger and the kind of irrational behavior which stirs the worst instincts in the hearts of men. In their anger they put a premium on violence, nourish hatred, and give free reign to their desires for revenge. They attempt to crush the weak in order to advance their own tyranny.

The conspiracy against the Jews is formidable. The isolation of those in Jerusalem is (almost) complete. To be sure, the wall is being built and the breaches[2] are being closed, but what is this against such malignant forces?

[1] The text of verse 8 presents some difficulties. It is usually translated: "to cause confusion [lit., do wickedness] *in it*" (i.e., the city). This rendering is ungrammatical and a better suggestion would be to translate this section as follows: "to cause confusion *to me*" (i.e., to undermine Nehemiah's leadership). This offers a plausible solution to an otherwise difficult interpretive problem.

[2] The Hebrew text is picturesque. It reads quite literally that *"a bandage was applied"* to the walls of the city.

Adversity, however, tests the reality of one's faith and, as we shall see, nothing can prevent or hinder their prayers.

Facing the Crisis

As soon as Nehemiah becomes aware of the conspiracy, he takes immediate action. He records, "but *we* prayed to our God, and because of them we set a watch against them day and night." Once again, he shows how faith (i.e., prayer) and works (setting a watch) go together. He shows that prayer is not a substitute for action. He also takes adequate precautions by setting a watch! The spiritual preparation of the people becomes their inspiration as they undertake these added responsibilities. Furthermore, by using the pronoun "we" he reveals quite incidentally the effect of his own devout spirit on the people. Whereas previously (Nehemiah 4:4-5) he may have led them in prayer, here they are anxious to participate. And who can say how encouraged he was to find the people anxious to join him in bringing their problems before the Lord.

But then the unexpected happens!

As is so frequently the case, a change in the tactics of their enemies succeeds in undermining the resolve of the people. In spite of their renewed zeal the forces they face seem to be stronger than their awareness of spiritual realities. The cause of the deterioration of their morale is not immediately apparent. The first intimation Nehemiah has of a crisis takes the form of an ultimatum; and it comes from the most unlikely source—the men of Judah. Of Judah it has been written: "Your hand shall be on the neck of your enemies . . . Judah is a lion's whelp . . . who dares rouse him up? The scepter shall not depart from Judah, nor the ruler's staff from between his feet, until He [Christ] comes to whom it belongs" (Genesis 49:8-10).

The men of Judah said: "The strength of the burden bearers is failing, yet there is much rubbish; and we ourselves are *unable* to rebuild the wall."

To be sure, the *outward* cause of this ultimatum is exhaustion. The reduction of the number of workmen owing to the appointment of the guard, not to mention the longer hours, has increased the strain on those working inside the city.

As a wise leader Nehemiah does not accept this admission of

defeat at face value. He explores a little further and uncovers the real reason for the deterioration of morale. The "reason" the men of Judah have given him is only a rationalization. It is designed to make their failure look respectable. It is a defense to save them from losing face before the others. As is so often the case, the real reason for wanting to quit is *internal*. It comes directly from "the Jews who lived near their enemies" (Nehemiah 4:12). They have picked up the gossip which Sanballat has "leaked" to them and bring it into the city each day when they arrive for work. "The enemy," they say, "will come upon us from every place where we may turn." We are completely surrounded. We don't stand a chance!

The ruse of Sanballat and his coconspirators is successful. They intended to make the people afraid and destroy their *esprit de corp;* and they succeeded. Fear undermined the Jews' resolve and eroded their confidence in Nehemiah.

When Nehemiah finds the real reason for the collapse in the morale of the leaders, he rebukes them. "Do not be afraid of them," he says; "remember the Lord who is great and awesome, and fight for your brothers, your sons, your daughters, your wives, and your houses."

The key to Nehemiah's successful handling of this crisis lies in his ability accurately to diagnose what is wrong. He finds the problem to be internal rather than external. Only a few days before, these same people have joined him in prayer when danger threatened. They previously had seen God take a hand in their affairs. This had given them confidence. Then a new kind of threat arose. It was more subtle than the first, and they were unsuspecting. They kept a watch over the city walls, but did not heed what they were hearing. Quite unwittingly they were allowing the enemy subtly and systematically to brainwash them. They failed to realize that when doubt invades the soul, it inevitably leads to despair. When this happens, failure is only a few steps away.

In responding to this new development, Nehemiah addresses himself to the main issue: fear! He knows that there is a fear (a reverential awe) of the Lord which is healthy (Deuteronomy 5:29; 6:2; 13:4; Proverbs 14:26-27; 19:23; 29:25; Jeremiah 32:39). He knows that when God is held in reverence (as the proper fear-Object) all of life is brought into perspective.

Nehemiah, however, is also aware that there are times in life when some external threat causes us to fear someone or something else (Sanballat).[3] This becomes an improper fear-object. The result is a conflict between what is proper and what is improper. The reason for this inner conflict is that we have attributed to this false fear-object the characteristics of almightiness and impendency.[4] The result is weakness, timidity, and eventual capitulation.

The way in which Nehemiah handles this situation is most instructive. He first rebukes the Jews: "Do not be afraid of them." Then he encourages them: "Remember the Lord." Finally he motivates them: "Fight for those things you hold dear." In a word, he challenges their emotions.

It should be remembered that the Jews had come to Nehemiah with a contrived reason for their inability to continue to build the wall. The real reason might never have surfaced had Nehemiah not been a keen observer of human nature. He discerned their uneasiness and, looking beneath the rationalization, found the real reason. Then, as a wise leader, he tackled the real reason, not their rationalization.

Knowing how to diagnose a decline in morale and being able effectively to encourage and motivate our co-workers—whether in a large corporation or in a church, in a hospital or on the mission field—is one of the important factors in successful leadership. But we must be in touch with those with whom we work. This is the only way we can counteract negative influences. We must be visible. And with visibility must come accessibility. In our contemporary society, with so many demands being made on each one of us, we are all prone to overlook the importance of the personal dynamic in leadership. In an unsigned editorial in *Supervisory Management*, the writer pointed out that "a basic function of a good leader is to inspire people to their best efforts. The man who concentrates only on details, on cost figures or on technical matters, may become an expert, but not a leader. Experts know what should

---

[3] An example of an improper fear-object may be found in Numbers 13:21-29. The sons of Israel become afraid of what they might encounter in Canaan. Their proper fear-Object should have been the Lord (Numbers 13:30—14:25,36-37). Nehemiah was surely familiar with this and other incidents in the history of his people.

[4] Impendency—the power to take over control of our lives.

be done; leaders know what should be done and *how to get peo- ple to do it."* A leader must be able to rebuke, encourage, and motivate others.

In the passage before us, Nehemiah undertakes the task of cheering the dispirited workers. Their own leaders are of no help. Sufficient to say that Nehemiah is able to overcome their fear by means of his own enthusiasm. His enthusiasm is kept alive throughout the entire building program by the God-given ideal that has taken hold of his imagination, and by the confidence he has in the Lord and in himself. Because of his unshakable convictions, he is able to challenge those of lesser commitment and determination. His confidence in the God of the covenant gives him an "infectious optimism," which is the very essence of successful motivation. It also enables him to persevere in the face of difficulty and to radiate confidence. He can rely on moral and spiritual principles and resources even when he is not sure what his enemies will do next.

The Pursuit of Ideals

In the course of time the threat of an attack on Jerusalem becomes very real (Nehemiah 4:15-20).

When Sanballat realizes that his subtle psychological warfare is no longer having the desired effect, he plans an all-out offensive. Word of this no doubt comes to Nehemiah through his ally in Samaria. To prepare for the attack, Nehemiah has all the workers armed. Men are stationed at strategic places behind the wall and in the exposed sections. During these days work on the wall ceases.

The cessation of building operations may have been regarded by some as a sign of failure. Nehemiah, however, realizes that "liberty does not consist merely in the rights of men, but in the translation of those declarations into definite actions." The work on the wall has to be suspended temporarily while the people safeguard their freedom.

Nehemiah's arrangements for the military protection of Jerusalem converts the entire city into an armed camp. Residents from the surrounding areas are required to stay in the city instead of returning to their homes at night. This insures that all personnel will be available in case of an attack. It also cuts down on the ease with which Sanballat and Tobiah are able to disseminate their propaganda and discourage the people.

Nehemiah's counter offensive meets with such success, that he is able to write: "And it happened that when our enemies heard that it was known to us and that God had frustrated their plan [of attack], *then all of us returned to the wall, each to his own work.*" From this time onward, the amount of work accomplished each day slows down. Half of the force stand on guard, while the others work. The workers are armed. A trumpeter is positioned near Nehemiah and is ready to summon everyone in the event of a surprise assault. In spite of the fact that they are hampered by these precautions, and are also tired and working extra guard duty at night, the work continues!

The Cutting Edge

Nehemiah concludes this chapter with a summary. In verses 21-23, he recounts the events of these pressurized days and tacitly shows us the reason for his success. The basic element of his success may be found in his *identification* with the Jews (Nehemiah 4:23). He was willing to endure the same privation, face the same danger, and suffer the same hardships. He was one with them in the work! The temporary setback experienced when the building of the wall stopped did not deter him.[5] He was always moving forward.

Leaders of today may learn from the way in which Nehemiah handled himself during these tense, trying times. When a difficult situation arose he faced it objectively. He was sensitive to the needs of those within Jerusalem as well as to the plots and schemes of those without. While he may have regretted the interruption of the building program, he nevertheless faced each new situation realistically. He reordered his priorities and adjusted his strategy accordingly. Neither pressure nor tension caused him to deviate from his ultimate objective.

The basic undergirding of Nehemiah's life was his *faith*. His faith was the vital seed which inspired others and produced a

[5] Nehemiah's ability to reorder his priorities will be seen again in the next chapter.

harvest of achievements. Because of his faith, he was able to motivate the Jews. He knew that to give up was to count God out. God had allowed Sanballat and the others to oppose the work. Should he doubt God's providence? Doubt was a one-way street leading to failure! Faith, on the other hand, created a positive expectation which he was sure would culminate in the realization of his plans (Hebrews 11:6).

In the same way that Nehemiah's faith linked him to the Source of strength, his faith also became the ground of his confidence. It gave him the courage to persevere. He had the confidence that what he was doing was what God wanted done. As a result he could rise above the disturbing conflicts which surrounded him.

Faith can give us a sense of purpose as well. It can give us the confidence to approach each new day with reliance upon the Lord. The thrill and challenge which came to Nehemiah can be ours as well when we realize that we are vitally involved in God's work. As the Apostle Paul said, "whatever you do in word or deed, do all in the name of the Lord Jesus, giving thanks through Him to God the Father" (Colossians 3:17). This principle remains true whether our work is the building of a wall, serving in a cafeteria, or sitting behind a typewriter.

Nehemiah's faith in the One who had called him to undertake this task also gave him enthusiasm. And his enthusiasm helped him turn a potentially disastrous situation into a unifying situation. Without enthusiasm, the greatest plans in the world are subject to failure. With enthusiasm, no task is too great and no opposition too formidable. As a result of Nehemiah's own inner dynamic, the tired, fearful workers were motivated to accomplish what seemed to all intents and purposes to be impossible.

But how do we define this "inner dynamic"? Is it one of the intangibles that we must be born with to be a successful leader, or can we develop it?

Enthusiasm is not a magical something that we either have or must forever do without. It is based on two important qualities—truth and character. Nehemiah, we find, was committed to the truth. By following the truth, he developed the quality of character so necessary in a capable leader. When he came to Jerusalem, he was able to make truth of what God wanted for His people the focus of a common purpose, and his character became the important dynamic which inspired (i.e., enthused) the Jews to follow him with confidence. Effective leadership is based upon both of these qualities, truth and character.

Finally, Nehemiah triumphed because of his confidence in the Lord. By way of contrast, his opponents were again faced with ignominious defeat.

TIME FOR REFLECTION

1. Nehemiah is again called upon to withstand anger (see
    Nehemiah 4:1b and 7b). The Hebrew word for "anger" means
    "to burn (as with fire), to be consumed." Add to this the
    emphasis of the word *very* and you have some indication of
    the intensity of feeling displayed by the "enemies of the
    Jews." An angry person is always right in his own eyes. He
    may act irrationally or vindictively. How did Nehemiah and
    those in Jerusalem handle the new situation as it developed?
    To what extent did they assume responsibility for the reaction
    of those in Samaria and elsewhere? Was the response of
    Nehemiah and those working on the wall sufficient for and
    appropriate to the situation? Why?

2. Notice the effect fear produces (Nehemiah 4:10-12). Of what
    were the workers afraid? Why had the workers allowed their
    confidence to be undermined? What precautions should the
    workers have taken?

3. All leaders face discouragement—in themselves and in their
    subordinates. How did Nehemiah handle this problem?
    Based on Nehemiah 4:7-23, what would you consider to be
    the dynamics of discouragement? (Compare your response
    with the analysis at the end of this study.) What can we learn
    from Nehemiah that will be of help to us when we are faced
    with a similar predicament?

4. The crisis brought about by the threat of Sanballat and his
    associates produced an internal problem. The people were
    afraid. They attributed to this coalition two important
    attributes that properly belong to God: almightiness (the
    power to do them harm) and impendency (the power to take
    away their autonomy). How did Nehemiah overcome their
    fear (Nehemiah 4:14)? Was Nehemiah successful? Is his
    approach a healthy way to deal with someone who is fearful?

    To what do you attribute Nehemiah's ability to encourage
    these dispirited people? Is it important for leaders today to
    refocus a fearful person's attention on spiritual resources?
    When we are dealing with an unsaved person do we have an

opportunity for witness? What emotional rationale did Nehemiah give in order to motivate the people to continue the work? Was this motivation intrinsic or extrinsic? What benefits did it have over the other method of motivation?

Something to think about: Abraham was also a man of faith. In the book of Genesis we read that when he began his odyssey, he and those who were with him "set out for the land of Canaan; and into the land of Canaan they came" (Genesis 12:5). God was faithful. He accomplished what He had promised. The fact that God keeps His promises does not mean that Abraham's life (or yours or mine) was immune from trial, or the need for planning. It does mean that God is sovereign and that He will accomplish His will concerning us if we remain faithful to Him and do not allow our faith to be eclipsed by sudden fear.

Suggested analysis in response to Question 3:

(1) Fatigue played a part in their emotional state. They were tired. This became an emotional "string" which their enemies could use to their own advantage. A contributing factor was also the fact that work on the wall had become routine. The newness of the project had worn off. Their endurance was being tested.

(2) They had lost their vision. The benefits of independence and the dignity it would bring had disappeared. In its place they could see only the problem: "There's so much dirt. . . ." The work of hauling all the dirt away seemed endless.

(3) They lost their confidence. Success seemed out of their grasp. They concluded, "We can't go on" (Nehemiah 4:10).

(4) They felt very insecure. No longer trusting in the Lord, they succumbed to fear.

7

EXPECT THE IMPOSSIBLE

Nehemiah 5:1-13

Early theories of group leadership claimed that a person could function as a leader if he had the personality that made it possible for the members of a group to achieve their objective under his supervision. Later, research psychologists enlarged upon this view. They believed that leadership behavior consisted in actions that were functionally related to goal achievement or directly connected to the maintenance and strengthening of the group. This theory, however, did not provide for "role differentiation" within groups, particularly where certain members initiate more than their share of communication. The result of this type of situation directly influences group attitudes and performance.

In combining these ideas it became common to talk of Theory "X" and Theory "Y" leaders. It is preferable, however, to speak of "task specialists" and "social-emotional experts." These terms describe different leadership roles.

In Nehemiah 5, a situation arose that called for the skills of a social-emotional expert—one who could maintain group morale and harmony—and, at the same time, help ease the tensions arising from certain working conditions.

Of all the tensions that operate in society, few are as dangerous as those which exist between the affluent and the underprivileged. James, our Lord's brother, wrote of it (see James 1:1-13), and it continues to plague our churches today. But churches are not the only ones facing this problem. Leaders in business and industry know that it is not uncommon for a spiral movement to develop that constantly increases the explosive contrast between prosperity and poverty.

But how is an administrator to handle a situation like this?

As we turn to the passage before us, we see that the man who succeeds in handling circumstances of this nature is one who sees people as people. To him they have value. They are not regarded as things to be used or exploited. He also has a clear view of reality and is not afraid to point out the truth, however painful it might be. Furthermore, he must be able to assume responsibility, and engender in the workers a new togetherness. As we found in an earlier chapter, at the heart of this kind of leadership there lies a commitment to the truth. Without this commitment extremism is sure to be the result.

Rich Man, Poor Man

In Nehemiah 5, we read: "Now there was a great outcry of the people and of their wives against their Jewish brothers. For there were those who said, 'We, our sons and our daughters, are many; therefore let us obtain grain that we may eat and live.' And there were others who said, 'We have mortgaged our fields, our vineyards, and our houses that we may obtain grain because of the famine.' Also, there were those who said, 'We have borrowed money for the king's tax on our fields and our vineyards.' And now our flesh is like the flesh of our brothers, our children like their children. Yet behold we are forcing our sons and our daughters to be slaves, and some of our daughters have been forced into bondage already, and it is not in the power of our hands to help them, because our fields and our vineyards belong to others."

The complaint of the working class is heightened by the presence of women. Their shrill voices add to the intensity of the meeting. Nehemiah finds himself faced with a situation that can easily get out of hand.

But why are these people thus impoverished? Only ninety years earlier, the first of their number to return from exile had come back amply supplied with worldly goods (Ezra 1:5-11). Those who chose to remain in Babylon had given liberally to their support. Even Cyrus had opened the doors of his treasury and lavished upon them "vessels of gold and silver." Further-more, they left the land of their captivity mounted on asses, horses, camels, and mules (Ezra 2:66-67). Additional evidence

of their wealth may be found in the fact that many of the Jews
paneled their new homes—something previously reserved for
kings (Haggai 1:4). At the building of the Temple, they had given
extravagantly towards its embellishment (see Nehemiah
7:71-72). Only thirteen years earlier (458 B.C.), Ezra had
brought a second group of colonists from Babylon. Artaxerxes I
and his counselors had contributed freely toward their needs
(Ezra 7:15-16), and large gifts were constantly coming from
their wealthy relatives in Babylon (Zechariah 6:10-11).

Then why this outcry? What could have caused such
poverty?

As we take a closer look at the internal affairs of the Jews,
we see that there are three distinct groups mentioned in these
verses.

The first to voice their grievances are the merchants and
laborers (Nehemiah 5:2). By their own admission they have
large families. In their rebuilding of the wall they have sustained themselves. Now, without an income, they are no longer
able to support those who are dependent upon them. Their
resources have been used up. The situation they face is bleak.
There is no way out of the impasse unless help is forthcoming.

The second group are farmers (Nehemiah 5:3). Their farms
are especially vulnerable to robber bands from the hill country
or Bedouin tribesmen from across the border. It was not uncommon for these people to anticipate a bumper crop, only to
have their harvest stolen from them by those who raided their
lands, or plundered their small villages.

In these straitened times, a farmer, to support his family,
would borrow money on his fields, or against his crops. The
rate of interest was exorbitant![1] If his crops failed,[2] or famine

[1] According to verse 11, interest was charged by the "loan sharks" at 1% per
month, or 12% per annum. This was excessively high in those days!
[2] The Prophet Haggai describes the condition of the people of Judah before the
time of Ezra and Nehemiah. Their materialism separated them from the Lord.
As a result, He began frustrating their expectations (Haggai 1:4-6,9-11; 2:16-19).
They sowed much but reaped little. They tried to enjoy life but never seemed to
be really happy. They "earned wages to put into a bag with holes" (i.e., they
could never get ahead and plan for the future. Something always came along to
eat up what they were trying to save). If the condition that Haggai describes
continued for any length of time, the situation of those in Judah could easily fit
the description given in Nehemiah 5:2-6.

came, or locusts decimated the land, then the "loan sharks" would take away his lands and sell his family into slavery (Nehemiah 5:5). This was plainly contrary to the Law (Deuteronomy 23:19-20; 24:10-13). A man could sell himself or his daughters into slavery (but not his sons!), and then only to the end of a sexennial (Exodus 21:2,7-11; Leviticus 25:39-41,54). In the seventh year, all slaves went free (Leviticus 25:10; Deuteronomy 15:16); and if the year of jubilee came before the end of the sexennial, all servitude ended. Furthermore, in time of drought or famine, a man's land could be mortgaged or sold to someone of the same tribe, but it always reverted back to its original owner at the jubilee (Leviticus 25:10,14-17,25-27).

This provision of manumission had been made by God. He planned for His people to be free. To be sure, the poor would always be numbered among them, but in His economy they would never become completely destitute. Even if compelled to mortgage their lands, or forced to sell themselves into slavery, it was to be only for a limited period of time. To make provision for the poor, the Lord had established that the rich were to lend to them (Deuteronomy 15:7-11) without charging interest (Exodus 22:25; Leviticus 25:36). But these wise provisions had become a dead letter. The sabbatical years had not been kept, and the year of jubilee had been ignored. Slaves were not released, debts were not canceled, the rich exploited the poor, oppression was rife, and injustice prevailed (see Isaiah 5:8; Habakkuk 1:3-4).

The third group Nehemiah listens to are having trouble with their taxes. Judah, like all other Persian provinces, had to pay taxes, partly in money and partly in produce. These were not generally felt to be oppressive, but the very nature of the economy, coupled with the overbearing policy of the rich, made even a small amount of taxation a grievous burden. These farmers had willingly given all they had to work on the wall, but some of the rich moneylenders had foreclosed on their mortgages and sold their children into slavery. When the people compared themselves with those who were exploiting them, they said in effect, "We too are human. We love our children as much as they love theirs. We are willing to work, but they have made life impossible by owning our houses, our land, and our crops. It is not in the power of our hands to repay what we owe and redeem our children from slavery" (Nehemiah 5:5).

Caring Enough to Confront

As Nehemiah reviews the situation, his first response is one of *anger*. He realizes that what is being practiced is contrary to the plain teaching of Scripture. He therefore takes issue [3] with the nobles and the rulers of the people. "You are exacting usury, each from his brother!" he says. This, however, was not the complaint of the people. Their outcry was totally different. They had complained of a shortage of food, of being forced to mortgage their lands, of slavery, and of taxation. But Nehemiah's response is to go to the heart of the problem. He does not deal with peripheral issues. Outward circumstances can easily be rectified, but unless the root cause is dealt with the problem will only recur. In evaluating the situation he has come to the conclusion that the basis of the whole matter is one of exploitation. He therefore contends with the nobles and the rulers.

Apparently Nehemiah's rebuke has no effect on the leaders of the people. They give him no reason to believe that they will change their conduct. In fact, their silence gives evidence of their intransigence. They seem ready for a power struggle. The priesthood (who should have challenged their conduct) have long since been won over to their side (Nehemiah 6:12,14; see 13:4,7-9), and no one has arisen in recent years to tell them that their business practices are not in accordance with the Word of God. Furthermore, they are many and united. Nehemiah needs their help if he is to build the wall. What can he do to oppose their combined strength and influence?

But Nehemiah sees things differently. He is a man of principle. He knows that if the people do not live in accordance with the teaching of God's Word, they cannot enjoy His blessing. Realizing that he will only weaken his position by restating his point, he convenes a great assembly against them. To do this, the work again has to stop. Then, in the presence of all the peo-

---

[3] The word *contend* (Nehemiah 5:7) denotes a conflict of opinion as well as a method of approach.

ple, he challenges the nobles to return to the Lord and order
their lives by the standard laid down in His Word. In his
rebuke, he tacitly shows that a leader must set an example. He
describes his own conduct and compares what he has been doing with what the nobles and rulers have done. This forces an
intentional polarization. The contrast between their conduct
becomes obvious. The leaders of the Jews are shamed into
silence when it becomes known that they have sold the people
of Judah into slavery. Their shame increases when it becomes
known that those whom they have sold "to the nations"
(Nehemiah 5:8) have been bought by Nehemiah.

Nehemiah then rebukes them for not acting in accordance
with "the fear of God" (i.e., in submission to His authority), and
invites them to join him in lending money and grain without interest to those who are in need. Here again he leads by example, for what he recommends is exactly what he and his servants have been doing all along (Nehemiah 5:10).

The greed and heartlessness of the rulers has been adequately exposed. Their lack of concern for their own people
has been dealt with. In responding to Nehemiah's challenge,
they indicate their willingness to help those whom they have
heretofore exploited.

This willingness to lend money and grain without interest
represents a dramatic step in the right direction. It does not,
however, right the previous wrongs. A man of lesser stature
than Nehemiah might have been tempted to be thankful for
what had been accomplished and be unwilling to "push his luck
too far." Nehemiah, however, is not yet finished. The Law had
been broken and they cannot expect God's blessing while continuing to disobey Him (see Deuteronomy 23:20). He therefore
says, "Restore, I pray you, this very day, their fields, their
vineyards, their olive groves, and their houses, also the one
hundredth part of the money [i.e., the interest charged at the
rate of 1% per month] and of the grain, the new wine, and the
oil that you are exacting from them" (Nehemiah 5:11).

The nobles and rulers of the people have been silenced by
Nehemiah's example. They are overawed by his courage, and
agree to do as he asks. Nehemiah then takes a promise from
them in the presence of the priests. In keeping with the imagery
of the Near East he shakes out the front of his cloak in a sym-

bolic gesture, illustrating what God will do to the person who goes back on his word.

The response of the people is gratifying. They know that Nehemiah is on their side. His handling of the situation is just and equitable. Inspired by his godly qualities they give expression to sincere praise.

Thus a day begun with oppression and sorrow ends with rejoicing.

Our Convulsive Era

These verses contain important principles for today's leaders. Our era is one of continued depersonalization. People feel more like things than individuals of worth. In our economy, many corporations exploit those whom they hire. Their primary concern seems to be centered in pleasing the stockholders. Something very similar happens in Christian institutions. Those who willingly give of their time and ability, of their income and resources, have more and more demands made of them by the administration, with less and less appreciation. By way of contrast, those office managers and church leaders who have the ability to keep their personnel happy, also have more efficient and more productive departments. The key to this kind of effective leadership is found in Nehemiah's example.

In surveying this passage we notice, first, that the people had come to Nehemiah at a most inopportune time. He was busy building a wall and their "drop everything, we quit" attitude brought the work to a grinding halt. Worse still, others might become disgruntled as a result of their complaining spirit.

Nehemiah, however, shows us how to handle this kind of situation. He was prepared to stop and listen. He saw the complainers as people, not as statistics; and they were more important than his production schedule. As he listened he found that they were hurting inside. He knew from long experience that people who are deeply concerned over some personal misfortune or hardship cannot give of their best. He, therefore, encouraged them to air their grievances.

Secondly, Nehemiah probed beneath the surface issues to

the real cause of their predicament. Had he not done so he would have attacked the "fruit" of the problem and left the "root" untouched. This would have paved the way for the same kind of trouble to crop up again—only in different ways and in different places. Eventually he would have had to diversify his efforts in order to take care of a multitude of social ills; and this would have resulted in the obscuring of his goals. Only by attacking the real issue was Nehemiah able to rectify the problem.

Thirdly, Nehemiah had the courage to act. Many leaders see clearly what needs to be done, but lack the fortitude necessary to confront those responsible for the trouble. Nehemiah evaluated the problem in the light of the Word of God and called upon the leaders to conform to His revealed will.

Finally, he shows us the need for persistence.

In analyzing what this able executive did we see that the dynamics of effective leadership involve the skills of a task leader as well as a social-emotional expert. The task leader must be able to coordinate the efforts of the group, insure cooperation, commend honest effort, see that each task is completed satisfactorily, and provide for open lines of communication between employee and employer. The skills of a social-emotional expert are not difficult to uncover. Basically, they involve a willingness to *listen*, the ability to *probe the real issues* of a problem, the courage to take definite *action*, and the *persistence* to see matters through to a fitting conclusion.

ANGER . . . AND HOW TO HANDLE IT!

Anger as an emotion concerns all of us. We all, at one time or another, become frustrated and resentful. Society, however, frowns on those who cannot control their feelings. For this reason, some project their anger and blame other people for the way they feel. Others try to maintain a semblance of control when in public, only to take out their resentment in private on their spouses or their children. Still others work off their frustration in competitive sports or household duties. The majority of us, however, repress our emotions and soon forget the cause of our anger. But this, as we shall see, has serious aftereffects.

Anger is not necessarily sinful. The Apostle Paul recognized the inevitability of anger as an emotion when he wrote: "If you are angry, be sure that it is not out of wounded pride or bad temper. Never go to bed angry—don't give the devil that sort of foothold [so that he obtains control over you]" (Ephesians 4:26-27 Phillips).

But how may we handle anger so that we are not drawn into sin?

Anger becomes sinful when we lose control of ourselves (James 1:19-20; Galatians 5:19-21) or harbor resentment in a revengeful way (Romans 12:17-21). There is a moment of time in which we decide either to let go of our self-control or to maintain it in a grudging way. The result is conduct or attitudes not consistent with the Holy Spirit's constant control.

In Nehemiah 5, we see how a godly man handled anger. The example he set is one from which we may draw important lessons for the real-life situations we face.

From the very beginning the building of the wall of the city of Jerusalem was beset by hardships. Nehemiah's task was made even more difficult because the volunteers had left their farms and other forms of employment to work on the wall. While engaged in the work, they had no other means of support.

In the midst of the building operations, there was a great outcry of the workers and their wives. They were being oppressed and exploited by the wealthy who stood to gain the most from the fortification of the city.

Into the Arena

Nehemiah's response to this outcry is as instructive as he was honest. "Then I was very angry," he says.

The first thing Nehemiah did was admit his anger. He did not excuse it, ignore it, or minimize it. He did not try to project it on others or blame them for the way he felt. He didn't try to repress it. Had he done so, he might ultimately have forgotten the incident; but the suppression of his feelings would have had a damaging effect on his personality.

In handling his anger as he did, Nehemiah sets us an important example. While we may become angry for different reasons, we have the same options he had. We may, for example, try to excuse our frequent outbursts. One person may say, "But that's the way I'm made!" not realizing that he is projecting the blame for his actions on to God, his parents, and his environment. The truth of the matter is that, unlike Nehemiah, he is not prepared to admit that he is angry. He automatically equates anger with sin, and does not understand that the evil in anger comes from harboring it or desiring revenge.

A second reaction is a more blatant projection of anger. The direct assertion is, "You make me act this way!" Here, again, there is an attempt on the individual's part to dodge the full implication of his emotional involvement. He attempts to justify himself. He implies that others are to blame for his loss of temper. Such an attitude is childish.

Others, realizing the immaturity of blaming people, situations, or circumstances for the way they act and feel, refrain from giving any outward expression of their resentment. They do not want to lose face with or estrange their peers. As a result, they repress their anger. In time, they forget the reason for their hostility, but become critical in spirit, overly defensive, competitive, egotistical, and even depressed. Their attitudes become warped, and their interpretation of the motives of others becomes distorted.

Nehemiah did none of these things. He admitted his anger. Even though it was brought about by circumstances over which he had no control, he did not blame others for the way he felt. Having admitted that he was "very angry" he was then in a position to deal with his feelings and respond to the situation.

The Need for Elbow Room

In recalling the incident, Nehemiah says, "and I consulted with myself." He didn't do what so many of us do when we become angry, namely gossip about it. Sometimes when we ask others for their opinion we really want to tell them our story—bit by bit, and with pretended reluctance—but so as to impugn the integrity of the person whom we believe has wronged us.

Nehemiah was secure enough in his relationships that he did not need to justify himself in the eyes of others. He was primarily interested in what God thought of the situation. By "consulting with himself" he avoided the temptation of maligning others and steered clear of the sin connected with criticism (James 1:19-20,26).

By thinking the matter through, Nehemiah gave himself time to evaluate the situation and decide on a course of action. Had he not engaged in this introspection, he might have acted hastily and indiscreetly. All too often we fail to evaluate the occasion of our anger, and decide on our responsibility in the matter. By carefully weighing the circumstances surrounding our frustration or resentment we can resolve our part in the conflict. Only then are we in a position to tackle the problems others have.

Sensitive Confrontation

Having given himself time to gain perspective, Nehemiah then confronted those whom he believed to be in the wrong. He had thought through the issues and arrived at a decision. He saw clearly what needed to be done and took immediate action. "He contended with the nobles and the rulers."

So often, when we think through issues in an objective way, we lack the courage openly to confront those with whom we disagree. Satisfied that we are in the right (at least in our own eyes), we settle down complacently. Only under extreme provocation do we discuss the cause of our resentment with those with whom we are offended. It is easy to find reasons for not doing what we know needs to be done.

Having made his decision, Nehemiah boldly confronted the hierarchy of Jerusalem and explained the inconsistency in their conduct. Then he convened a great assembly and, after detailing the charges against them, gave his opponents an opportunity to reply. But "they were silent and could not find a word to say."

A Time to Mend

With all the people fully cognizant of the issues, Nehemiah then moved to bring the entire affair to a satisfactory conclusion. He became conciliatory. "Please, leave off this usury," he said. "Please give back to them this very day their fields."

Was this attempt at uniting the people a sign of weakness?

Did Nehemiah fear the consequences of his action? Had he been too bold in what he said? Is this the reason he softened his statements? By no means! Nehemiah was conciliatory, but without compromising his position. He was a man of unquestioning integrity; and he addressed the nobles and rulers of the people from a position of strength. Instead of lowering his standards, he invited them to join him.

This move toward conciliation is where so many of us fail. If we have the courage of our convictions and openly confront those with whom we disagree, we frequently part company the worse for our encounter. Then, after the altercation, we smirkingly congratulate ourselves on our success, while the other party goes off determined that next time the outcome will be different.

In the very move toward conciliation there is an inherent danger. Nehemiah knew human nature too well to place confidence in verbal assurances. He was not prepared to allow time to dull the memory or let changing circumstances alter the intent of anyone's agreement.

Those who have been in similar situations know how easy it is for some people to wait until the details of an agreement are forgotten and then revert to their former ways. Others, when challenged with the discrepancy between their verbal compliance and their subsequent conduct, are quick to say, "But I didn't understand it in that way." Nehemiah was a realist. He was not prepared to leave things to chance. He required a stronger form of commitment—something in writing (or its equivalent). The nobles and rulers complied with Nehemiah's demand and *formally* committed themselves to the course of action they had promised.

Then a remarkable thing happened. "All the assembly said 'Amen [so be it]!' And they praised the Lord."

This result is important. It shows that God can be glorified when we handle things in the proper way.

TIME FOR REFLECTION

1. In what way did Nehemiah listen to the expressions of discouragement voiced by the different groups of people? How did he probe the source of the problem? What does his analysis indicate about his knowledge of the Bible? Did he feel that the teaching of Scripture was relevant to life? What evidence is there that he practiced the precepts taught in those portions of the Word that were available to him?

2. What was Nehemiah's response to the expressions of discouragement? How did he feel toward the people who were being oppressed? In what way did Nehemiah use his own emotion to good advantage? What "safeguards" regulated his anger?

3. How did Nehemiah go about righting the wrongs that had been committed? What value is there in *consulting with oneself* (in the Hebrew, "to counsel oneself, to give oneself advice")? How do you think the people felt when Nehemiah championed their cause? Was this the first time he had done something like this?

4. How would you describe Nehemiah's plan of action? (Note: Nehemiah's reprimand was based on the facts, not on emotion. His charges were presented logically and without ambiguity.) Of what benefit was Nehemiah's face-to-face confrontation with those who had violated God's law? What was the effect (a) on the nobles and the officials, (b) on the people?

Something to think about: Consider the following excerpt from J. C. Penney's article, "Life Must Be Faced Squarely," in the *Christian Herald*:

The test of the individual and his greatness is not the magnitude of the problems he faces, but how well he adjusts himself to the conditions in which he finds himself, and solves his problems. This matter of adjustment is a complex one, and you will never find any simple answer that will

cover all the decisions you must make. Each day brings with
it new challenges of your ability, and your desire to live in
harmony with those about you.

8

PATTERN OF THE PAST

Nehemiah 5:14-19

What sets one man apart and marks him a success, whereas another of equal ability, if given the same opportunity, fails? Why are some men able to win the confidence of those whom they lead, while others are unable to rally men to their cause?

Some years ago I had the pleasure of working under a manager whose career had been marked by success. From the time he took office, everything improved—attitudes, efficiency, production. His standards were high, and he required the most of each employee. Although he was very demanding, it was a delight to come to the office. Minor power struggles ceased. Bickering in the typists' pool ended. Cooperation became the watchword. Everyone knew exactly where he stood and what was expected of him.

As I viewed the respective departments, each employee seemed to be much happier. Promotions were more frequent. The staff seemed to have taken on the attitude of the new manager.

From this experience it would be easy to jump to the conclusion that PMA—a positive mental attitude—was the key. Such, however, was not the case. There was something far more basic at work in the lives of all the people. It was a spirit of forthrightness and honesty. Everyone, from the assistant manager to the custodian, knew what was required of him. His duties were clear and his personal integrity had to be above question. And with personal trustworthiness came on-the-job reliability.

The importance of integrity has been borne out by the late Dwight D. Eisenhower. He said, "In order for a man to be a leader he must have followers. And to have followers, he must have their confidence. Hence the supreme quality for a leader is unquestionable integrity. Without it, no real success is possible, no matter whether it is on a section gang, a football field, in an army, or in an office. If a man's associates find him guilty of phoniness, if they find that he lacks forthright integrity, he will fail. His teachings and actions must square with each other. The first great need, therefore, is integrity and high purpose."

Nehemiah's unquestioned integrity helped him cope with opposition from without and handle strife within. It provided him with courage and undergirded his conduct.

The Heart of the Matter

In our previous chapter, we found that the work of rebuilding the wall of the city again had to stop. Justice had to be restored. The rich had been exploiting the poor and their greed finally precipitated a crisis. It required the resolute bravery of Nehemiah before the elite of Jerusalem would change their ways. But was boldness enough? To tell the rulers to "do as I say, but not as I do" would have produced disastrous consequences. In order successfully to resolve the problem, Nehemiah's own conduct had to be above reproach. But what inner dynamic brought all of Nehemiah's life into conformity with the truth? And how did his integrity help him face this new crisis?

Nehemiah explains the *sine qua non* of his own attitude in 5:15. "But I did not do so, because of the fear [i.e., the reverential awe] of my God."

The "fear of the Lord" is described as the foundation of right conduct (Psalm 111:10; Proverbs 1:7). Standing in awe of the Lord combines two opposite ideas: repulsion and attraction.

Whenever a person enters the presence of God, there is a feeling of unworthiness. This was Isaiah's experience when he had a vision of the glory of God filling the Temple (Isaiah 6:1-5). And Peter expressed the same sentiment when he suddenly recognized *who* Jesus was (Luke 5:8). These men illustrate the idea of *repulsion*—man wanting to flee from God's presence. They realized that God is holy, and that they were sinful. The result was they were overawed by (i.e., feared) God.

In the "fear of the Lord," there is also the element of *attraction*. God is the all-powerful One who meets us in our need and becomes our Helper. His love is such that we are instinctively drawn to Him. We realize that we are the objects of His grace. This gives us confidence as we approach Him (Hebrews 4:16). Our awareness of His presence is followed by confession of our unworthiness (see Isaiah 6:5-7), and submission to His will. This is what Isaiah experienced when he said, "Here am I; send me" (6:8).

The root idea in the "fear of the Lord"[1] is holiness (2 Corinthians 7:1). God says, "Be holy for I am holy" (1 Peter 1:15-16). The essence of holiness is separation—separation *from* the world's system *to* God's standards and values (Deuteronomy 6:4-19). The worldly people of Nehemiah's day could exploit their own people because they did not live in reverential awe of God. On the other hand, Nehemiah could say: "I did not do so because of the fear of my God." Real reverence for God leads to uprightness of life (Proverbs 8:13). It brings us to a place in our experience where we gladly do His will (Ecclesiastes 12:13), and it places us in a position where we can enjoy the blessings of His love (Deuteronomy 5:29; Psalm 147:11).[2]

It was the "fear of the Lord" that kept Joseph from committing adultery with Potiphar's wife (Genesis 39:9). It was

---

[1] Different doctrinal systems have exaggerated either the *fear* or the *love* of God. The errors which have grown up around these teachings affect one's happiness, sense of well-being, and ability to respond to God's grace. Exaggerating the *fear* of God results in legalism (i.e., a set of rules, or a moral code) which becomes a standard. Whenever we have man-made rules (an improper fear-object), we have something akin to the setting up of a false deity or deities found in the ritual worship or superstitious beliefs of pagan religions. The same kind of things happen when there is an overemphasis on the *love* of God. Those who stress the love of God and ignore His other attributes, make a "god" for themselves who will condone their evil practices and not punish them for their sins (Romans 1:18-32). This leads to license and is similar to the sensual worship of many pagan religions. Both systems are found in modern movements where the stress is placed on either the creed (dogma) of the church or sect, or where there is an overemphasis on "liberty" and the redefining of ethical principles as in the case of theological "liberalism." In our conservative churches where there still is a strong evangelical emphasis and conduct is "prescribed," people frequently indulge in license in their fantasies. Only by holding God in the supreme position as Lord can we enjoy perfect freedom.

[2] Other passages which bear on this theme are Romans 8:15; Ephesians 3:12; 6:5-6; Acts 9:21; Colossians 3:2; 2 Corinthians 7:1; and Philippians 2:12.

reverence for the Lord which led Moses to renounce the af-
fluence of Egypt for the hardships of the wilderness (Hebrews
11:27). It was the fear of God that motivated Paul in his service
(2 Corinthians 5:11). And this same attitude enabled Nehemiah
to stand against the trend of the times and do a work for God's
glory. The "fear of the Lord" equipped him with a spirit of
integrity—of practical righteousness, which kept him from
being contaminated by the world's system of values.

The "fear of the Lord" also controlled Nehemiah's attitude
toward people. He had a real concern for them. Even in
Babylon he had bought Jews on the slave market and released
them. Now, in Jerusalem, his regard for them showed itself
when he took issue with those who were exploiting them. And it
was on account of the righteousness of his life that the leaders
were dumb, and could find nothing to say in answer to his
challenge (Nehemiah 5:8).

The reality of Nehemiah's reverence for God showed itself in
still another way. It revealed his priorities. He did not enrich
himself as the other governors had done. He tells us that for the
twelve years of his governorship, "neither I nor my kinsmen
have eaten the food of the governor. But the former governors
who were before me laid burdens on the people and took from
them bread [i.e., food], and wine besides forty shekels of silver
. . .we did not buy any land, and all my servants were gathered
to the work. Moreover, I fed at my table one hundred and fifty
Jews and officials, besides those who came to us [on official
visits] from the nations that were around us" (Nehemiah
5:14-17).

God had prospered Nehemiah in the service of Artaxerxes I,
and Nehemiah had sufficient to live on without taxing the people. He even drew on his private resources to maintain his staff
and entertain official guests. Obviously, possessions were less
important to him than the work of the Lord. His philosophy of
life was contrary to the world's system of values.

The Use and Abuse of Freedom

Nehemiah's example provides an important illustration of
the New Testament teaching on Christian liberty (Galatians
5:13-14). He had a right to expect the support of the people of

the province, but he purposely supported himself so as not to burden them.

Guidelines have been laid down in the Scriptures to help us make decisions about our liberty in Christ (see 1 Corinthians 8:1—11:1; Romans 14:1—15:13).[3] In the first place, liberty must be regulated by love. Our indulgence might cause someone who follows our example to err. This might easily have been true in Nehemiah's case. The disparity between the rich and poor was very great. The problem of whether or not to expect the support of the people could not be solved from the standpoint of knowledge and its rights. Instead it had to be determined by love and its obligations (1 Corinthians 8:1-13). And so, in the spirit of the New Testament, Nehemiah shows us that we too must be willing to refrain from what we regard as being rightly ours for the sake of others (1 Corinthians 8:9-13).

Furthermore, had Nehemiah accepted what was legitimately his (Nehemiah 5:14-15), it might easily have hindered the work of the Lord and undermined his influence. He therefore chose to become all things to all men that the work might continue to prosper (see 1 Corinthians 9). The other governors had abused their rights and had exploited the people. If Nehemiah had followed the precedent they set, it might have led to the awakening of desires for self-aggrandizement and/or possessions which, in turn, may have led him into sin (1 Corinthians 10:1-13). In our society the same desires may lead us to an incorrect use of our liberty with the result that, as with Lot (Genesis 19), we become identified with the world and engage in practices which are displeasing to God (1 Corinthians 10:14-22; Romans 14:13-23).

In the final analysis, two important criteria guide us in the use of our liberty. First, we should consider what is expedient and what edifies others. Secondly, we should do all things to the glory of God (1 Corinthians 10:23—11:1; Romans 15:1-13). This is what Nehemiah did. He assessed the situation and found it inopportune for him to demand a governor's remuneration. Any insistence on material support would have had a

---

[3] These important truths receive fuller explanation in Charles R. Erdman's delightful *Commentaries on the New Testament* (Philadelphia: Westminster Press, 1916-36). Individual volumes are available on "The Epistle to the Romans" and the "First Epistle to the Corinthians."

detrimental effect upon the people. With his eyes fixed on God and a future day of recompense, he prayed, "Remember me, O my God, for good, according to all that I have done for this people."

The Price of Success

Nehemiah then shows us the results of being motivated by the awe of the Lord. He says, "And I applied myself to the work of the wall . . . and all my servants were gathered there for the work" (Nehemiah 5:16). He was single-minded. He concentrated on one thing and one thing only. Unlike some modern corporation executives who try to keep in touch with the office from the golf course or their frequently visited vacation resorts, Nehemiah was personally involved in the work. He did not engage in any private ventures with their accompanying distractions. The charge of conflict of interest could not be laid at his door. Even his servants worked shoulder to shoulder with the rest of the people.

From Nehemiah's example an important principle of success emerges. In spite of all that has been written about "how to make it to the top," few writers seem to have realized the importance of single-mindedness. Yet, without singleness of purpose, there can be no adequate leadership. Whenever a leader is more interested in himself, his investments, and his personal ventures, than he is in his work, his employees soon learn about it. They, in turn, will lack motivation, their objectives will become indistinct, morale will sag, creativity will wane, and the best laid plans will come apart at the seams.

Pastors face the same problem. It is always easy to allow oneself to be sidetracked by some worthy social cause, teach in a nearby college (with extra remuneration), or supervise a building program. When this happens they will soon forget the singleness of purpose which made the Apostle Paul what he was (Philippians 3:13).

All this does not mean that a manager or a pastor must be on the job twenty-four hours a day, seven days a week. It does mean that he must have well-established priorities and concentrate on doing first things first. With personal integrity backing his dedication to the task at hand, he cannot help but be successful.

Nehemiah's single-mindedness was mingled with personal austerity. Those who, during his twelve years as governor, came to dine with him must have been appalled at the meager fare (Nehemiah 5:18). In contrast to the other governors who lived to the limit of their means, Nehemiah lived very frugally. Did this make him unhappy? It seems more likely that creative accomplishment brought him the self-satisfaction and personal fulfillment the other governors sought in ostentatious display. Nehemiah did what he knew God wanted done. This brought him the happiness and contentment others looked for in wealth and temporal things.

The Shadow of Destiny

Having given us some insights into his own personal motivation, Nehemiah closes with one of his brief prayers: "Remember me, O my God, for good, according to all that I have done for this people."

But why close in this way?

By concluding this section with prayer, Nehemiah provides us with one more insight into the working of his own heart. He was vitally involved in the present, but looking to the future. As with Abraham, he had his eyes set on "a city, whose builder and maker was God" (Hebrews 11:8-10). Following the example of Moses, he chose to "endure ill-treatment with the people of God, rather than to enjoy the passing pleasures of sin; considering the reproach of the Messiah [and His people] greater riches than the treasures of Egypt; for he was looking away to the reward" (11:25-26). With his eyes on the Lord, he could afford to forego the legitimate compensation which was rightfully his as governor in the "land beyond the river."

Nehemiah's attitude ably illustrates the truth of the song writer's words:

> This world is not my home,
> I'm just a-passin' through;
> My treasure's all laid up
> Somewhere beyond the blue.

He had a practical, vital, and effective relationship with

God. He was motivated by his knowledge of who God is, and strengthened by the assurance of what God can do. This relationship with God brought all of his life into conformity with the truth. It gave him an inner honesty which drew men to him. His integrity formed the basis of all of his relationships. It also gave him a balanced perspective on the world and his place in it. As a result he could relinquish his rights for the sake of the people and the work. His success came from his integrity and single-mindedness. He could forego temporal advantages because he sought God's approval alone. He was satisfied by the knowledge that his reward would come from the Lord.

TIME FOR REFLECTION

1. In Nehemiah 5:14-15 we are given a historic sidelight on Nehemiah's character and conduct while in office. He mentions his position for the first time. His example is important. It was consistent because he was motivated by the "fear of God." From a consideration of the following passages of Scripture, what do you believe should be our primary attitude toward the Lord: Leviticus 19:32; Deuteronomy 10:17-21; 1 Chronicles 16:25; Psalm 103:11,13,17; Proverbs 23:17; Isaiah 8:13-14a; Acts 9:31; 2 Corinthians 5:11; 7:1; Ephesians 5:21; Colossians 3:22; Hebrews 10:2? How may this attitude be carried over into the practical areas of life (e.g., Deuteronomy 6:13, worship)?

2. Do you think a verse like Proverbs 29:2 provides a sidelight on Nehemiah's administration? Why?

3. The temptation to use power to further one's own ends is always present. In what way did Nehemiah regulate his liberty so as not to oppress the poor or prejudice those who might be influenced by his example (Nehemiah 5:14-15)? Describe the manner in which Nehemiah became, as it were, "all things to all men" in order not to hinder the work (5:16a). If indulgence (e.g., enriching oneself), even in legitimate matters may endanger one's spiritual vitality, can we show that Nehemiah abstained from these pursuits (5:16b)? Encouragement to participate in subtle, though seemingly proper, "displays" of our success is all about us. What does Nehemiah's example teach us about avoiding such ostentation (5:17-18)? In what practical ways might drawing attention to yourself detract from Christ?

4. Nehemiah's primary concern was for what was best for the people. He knew, however, how quickly the masses forget the sacrificial service of their leaders. What motivated him to continue (Nehemiah 5:18; compare Hebrews 11:26)?

Something to think about: This comes from Floyd Hall, a past president of Eastern Air Lines. Interact with what he has to say.

The kind of guy who commands leadership is first of all the fellow who knows his business, and knows it so well that he exudes confidence. *Second, he has to be a thoroughly honest person, with himself and everyone else—not because some outside influence tells him, but because of an inner ethical sense that tells him right from wrong.* Finally, the natural leader must have a real appetite for accomplishment. He must have the ability to work hard for long periods of time, without breaking down mentally or physically under stress.

HANDLING OPPOSITION

WITHOUT COMING UNGLUED

Nehemiah 6:1-9

In his introduction to *Profiles in Courage*, the late John Fitzgerald Kennedy wrote, "A nation which has forgotten the quality of courage which in the past has been brought to public light is not likely to insist upon or reward that quality in its chosen leaders today." [1]

At the time these words were penned, President Kennedy was speaking of the American people. His observations, however, apply to men of any era, and it is not hard to find historic parallels to the conditions he was describing. Nehemiah, for example, possessed the qualities President Kennedy extolled. He did not serve his own desires, or even the people's. He bravely concentrated on doing what he believed God wanted done. He refused to pretend to have "extraordinary solicitude for the people, by flattering their prejudices, by ministering to their passions, and by humoring their transient and changeable opinions." He was influenced by the Word of God and followed God-given principles rather than a policy of expediency. This required courage.

The Consequences of Failure

As we turn to Nehemiah 6, we find that the wall has been completed although the gates (which were normally covered

---

[1] (New York: Harper, 1964), p.24.

with metal to prevent them from being burned in the event of a siege) have not yet been set up (6:1).

When Nehemiah's success is reported to Sanballat and Tobiah, to Geshem the Arab, and to the rest of the enemies of the Jews, they realize that their strategies have failed. They have underestimated their rival. They have made the mistake of thinking that their superior numerical strength, strategic location, and persistent harassment would be sufficient to halt the work. They have failed to take into account Nehemiah's spiritual resources (i.e., his God; see Nehemiah 2:20; 4:15,20; 6:16; etc.), and his personal resourcefulness.

Under ordinary circumstances, their strategies would probably have succeeded. The Jews were easily intimidated. On one occasion, they had even decided to quit the work. The key to the completion of the entire project was a person—Nehemiah. He encouraged the people to persevere and helped them work through their problems.

When Sanballat and his coconspirators realize that they had been outmaneuvered, outgeneraled, and outwitted by Nehemiah, they decide to attack him personally. They have a vendetta to settle. They resort first to *intrigue* (Nehemiah 6:1-4), then to *innuendo* (6:5-9), and finally to *intimidation* (6:10-14) to achieve their end. Their wounded pride will not be appeased until Nehemiah has been humiliated.

Rivals or Allies?

The jealousy of Sanballat and his associates first takes the form of *intrigue*. "Come," they say, "let us meet together at Chephirim."[2] This invitation, sent by letter, is a very astute move. Its very plausibility makes it deadly. Nehemiah's opponents are saying in effect, "Let's be friends. We've had our differences in the past. Now, however, you have accomplished what we never thought you could—you've built the wall of Jerusalem. We can't dispute your right to lead the Jews in the way you see fit. Whether we like it or not, we are neighbors; we have to get along with one another. Now that the wall has been

---

[2] The Hebrew contains the plural of *kaphar* and may refer to one of the villages on the Plain of Ono. On the other hand, *kepharim* may be the name of a place (see "Chephirah," Ezra 2:25).

finished, it is time for a summit conference. Select one of the villages in the Plain of Ono.[3] There we can meet together, resolve our differences, and plan for peaceful coexistence."

All of this sounds very magnanimous. The invitation promises an amicable settlement to their long-standing differences. It is made even more reasonable because the Jews are known to be hard-pressed, weary, and famine-stricken. The "conference" holds out hope of a truce, and will certainly be viewed by those in Jerusalem as an acceptable alternative to continued harassment. And what leader, with the social problems of the citizens on his shoulders, as well as the military responsibility for the protection of the city, would not respond to such a seemingly kind invitation? All of these supposed "plusses," however, overlook one important point: to what extent do you trust your enemy when he suddenly appears with "an olive branch" in his hand?

Historians will remember that the same kind of thing happened when the Pope promised John Huss safe conduct and fair treatment if he would attend the Council of Constance. These assurances did not prevent Huss from being seized and burned at the stake.

Nehemiah knew that without adequate leadership in Jerusalem, the people would speedily lapse back into their old ways. The priesthood was corrupt and the rulers avaricious. Exploitation would cause the morale to collapse, and dissension would again prevail. His place was in Jerusalem. The whole matter, therefore, became one of *priorities*.

Having come to a decision, Nehemiah sent his reply. "I am doing a great work and I cannot come down. Why should the work stop while I come down to you?" He knew that the gains made thus far must be secured. And he was already planning for "Phase Two" of the operation—the consolidation of the work.

Nehemiah also realized the danger of acceding to Sanballat's "invitation." By allowing himself to be drawn away from the security of the city, he would be exposing himself to the constant threat of assassination (Nehemiah 6:2; see Genesis 50:20; 1 Samuel 23:9; Esther 8:3). In fact, the more let-

[3] Situated toward Philistia where the Ashdodites, Sanballat's allies, are located.

ters Sanballat sent to Nehemiah the more his suspicions were confirmed.

Nehemiah's example shows us the importance of practical wisdom (see James 1:5-8). He knew what his priorities were and would not allow himself to be sidetracked from fulfilling them. His example also illustrates the need for adequate discernment (Hebrews 5:14), and the importance of tact. He did not antagonize Sanballat, but instead insisted on exercising his own autonomy. His ability to see the issues clearly and stand firm under pressure safeguarded him from succumbing to the wiles of his adversaries.

The Gospel of Judas

Having again failed to achieve their purpose, Sanballat and his coconspirators try a new strategy—*innuendo*. Sanballat sends his servant to Nehemiah with an open letter in hand, "It is reported among the nations, and Gashmu [the Arabic form of Geshem] says, that you and the Jews are planning to rebel; therefore you are building the wall. And you are to be their king, according to these reports. And you have appointed prophets to proclaim in Jerusalem concerning you, saying, 'There is a king in Judah!' And now it will be reported to the king [Artaxerxes] according to these words. So come now, let us take council together" (Nehemiah 6:6-7).

An open letter is the height of indignity. Sanballat knows that the contents of the letter will become public property. The charge of treason, even if unfounded and proven to be untrue, will be sufficient to impune Nehemiah's motives, cast aspersion on his integrity, and undermine his influence.

This attack on Nehemiah takes advantage of an important psychological principle. People are always quick to believe the worst about others. Think, if you will, of how quickly scandal spreads through an office or a church. The faintest hint at indiscreet behavior and the person concerned is pronounced guilty. To malign Nehemiah's motives is, therefore, very easy. The libel may be totally false, yet it is impossible for the victim of such calumny ever to clear his name with everyone who gives ear to the reports. The implication of Nehemiah's supposed treasonous activities is nothing less than attempted blackmail. The strength of their scheme lies in man's innate fear of reprisal. To anyone less heroic, their diabolic threat would have been overwhelmingly powerful. Nehemiah, however, faced their innuendo with commendable courage.

Some credence may even be given Sanballat's words in verse 7. With the renewal of national pride, someone may have preached on Zechariah's famous prophecy: "Behold, your King is coming to you; He is just and endowed with salvation, humble, and mounted on a donkey" (Zechariah 9:9). Even if such an expectation had been aroused, Zechariah's words were spoken of the coming Messiah, the Lord Jesus, not Nehemiah. If Sanballat latched on to some patriotic preacher's misguided statements and distorted them, then it only shows the extent to which ungodly men will go to deliberately misunderstand the obvious and twist the truth to serve their own ends.

Nehemiah's response to this attack is one of open denial. "Such things as you are saying have not been done, but you are inventing them in your own heart." His reply, however, is revealing. It shows that he is inwardly secure. He knows that in the final analysis, it is what God thinks of him that really matters. This places the attack on a different level. It adds a dimension to Sanballat's opposition which the Samaritan governor has persistently ignored. It brings God into the picture and links Nehemiah with a different world of reality! This new dimension enables him to endure the slander. To be sure, his influence has been undermined and his popularity poll has fallen. All along the rulers of the people have been looking for some weakness in his administration so that they may again assert their authority. Now, with the alienation of the people, and everyone aware of the fact that he is under attack, his task will be even more difficult.

In facing this new form of opposition Nehemiah has recourse to prayer. "But now [O God] strengthen my hands."

There are times in our lives when we too find that those whom we encounter malign our motives, alienate our subordinates, and weaken our hold on the situation. When this happens an *open denial* of what is plainly false and *prayer* are our only recourse.

I remember working on a faculty where one of the instructors could not stand anyone being more popular with the students than he was. The other faculty members constituted a threat to his identity. On one particular occasion tension developed between this instructor and one of his colleagues. The instructor's snide insinuations to the students ultimately led to the resignation of the other faculty member. Unfortunately, in this instance, open denial of the accusations was not matched with inward security; and the result was exactly what the instructor had hoped for—the removal of a colleague whom he felt was competing with him for student approval.

Personal security, as Maurice E. Wagner[4] has shown, comes from our relationship to the three Persons of the Godhead. Our relationship to God the Father gives us a sense of *belonging*. We are members of His family and are secure in our Father-child relationship. Our union with Christ the Son, gives us a sense of *worth*. God loved us so much that He sent His Son to die for our sins. With our redemption accomplished, God has made us joint heirs with Christ. This shows our value. Finally, the Holy Spirit's indwelling empowers us. We are made equal to every task (i.e., we are *competent*). These three things form the foundation of our inner security. This security helps us withstand the subtle innuendos of those who impune our motives and try to hinder the work that we are doing.

God's Gracious Provision

As we consider the way in which Nehemiah faced these attacks, we cannot help but notice two things: his discernment and his courage. When he first received the letters from Sanballat, he discerned their intrigue, and knew that they were planning to do him harm. As a result, he was able to avoid a potentially dangerous situation. His discernment also helped him see the issues clearly. He knew that the work in Jerusalem would suffer if he left it. He was aware of the need to consolidate the gains that had been achieved. His response to Sanballat's first attack was, therefore, one of firmly insisting on *his* right to make decisions based on *his* priorities.

But how did Nehemiah achieve this discernment?

[4] Maurice E. Wagner's book, *Put It All Together: Developing Inner Security* (1974), deserves careful reading!

Discernment comes from our personal exposure to the Word of God (Hebrews 5:13-14; see Proverbs 2:1-9). This involves more than merely reading a select passage of Scripture each day. It necessitates that we interact with what we read and apply the Word to our lives and to the situations we face.

As we have already seen, Nehemiah was a man of the Word. He had such an intimate knowledge of God's revelation, it is no wonder he had developed the ability to discern both good and evil.

David allowed the teaching of the portions of the Bible he possessed to permeate his thoughts. He could say: "Oh how I love Thy law! It is my meditation all the day. Thy commandments make me wiser than my enemies, for they are ever with me. I have more insight than all my teachers, for Thy testimonies are my meditation. I understand more than the aged, because I have observed Thy precepts. I have restrained my feet from every evil way. . . . From Thy precepts I get understanding; therefore I hate every false way" (Psalm 119:97-104).

The more we understand of the Bible, the better will we be able to discern the will of God. The more familiar we are with the Scriptures, the easier it will be for us to know the will of God (i.e., our priorities based on His leading) and act accordingly.

Secondly, when Nehemiah's enemies attacked his person he felt instinctively that his grip on the situation had been weakened. His response, therefore, was to deny the charge, commit the whole matter to the Lord, and relying on His strengthening, continue with the work. He did not spend time attempting to justify himself. By taking his problems to the Lord in prayer and leaving everything in His hands, he preserved his emotional stability. He was then able to continue with the construction and leave to the Lord the vindication of his person. Had he not done this he would have spent the rest of the day worrying about his problems . . . until they finally got the better of him.

Nehemiah's prayer life was important. It linked him with the world of reality. He knew that the Lord was the source of his strength (see Psalm 18:2,32,39; 19:14; 22:19; etc.). According to his custom, in the difficult and critical situations of life, he resorted to prayer. In this way he took care of the stress and strain of his high office.

In the instance before us, Nehemiah's brief ejaculatory prayer is simple, definite, and sufficient. He prayed that his hands might be strengthened. He sensed a need for an inward renewal of energy and a strengthening of his resolve. As with Isaiah the prophet, he knew that those who wait upon the Lord shall renew their strength (Isaiah 40:31; see Psalm 28:7-8; 29:11; 46:1). He therefore prayed that his hands might be strengthened so that the work might continue to prosper. Then he continued with the task God had entrusted to him. He was happy to leave his own reputation and future in the hands of the One to whom he had committed his life.

This secret of quiet confidence, of implicit trust in the Lord, and a willingness to do His will was the Apostle Paul's secret too. He wrote a letter (Ephesians) explaining to New Testament believers what Nehemiah's life so beautifully illustrated to the people of his day (see Romans 15:4; 1 Corinthians 10:11).

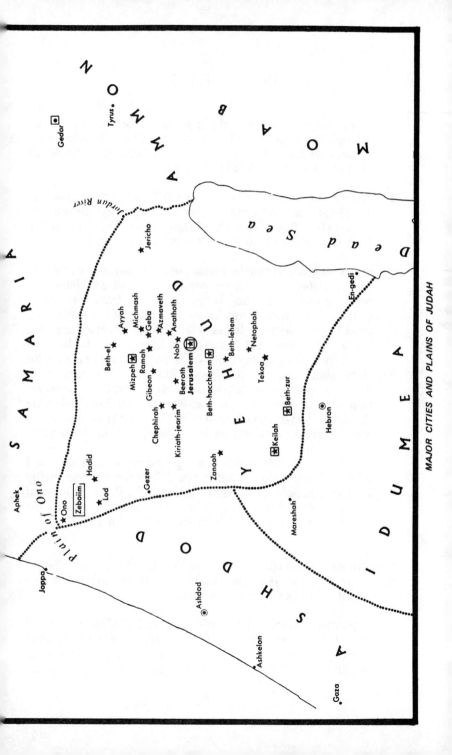

MAJOR CITIES AND PLAINS OF JUDAH

TIME FOR REFLECTION

1. The three major scenes of Nehemiah 6 form a unit. Read through the chapter and then make a chart. Provide each column with a heading describing in your own words the kind of opposition Nehemiah faced.

2. What was the purpose behind Sanballat's letters (Nehemiah 6:1-4), the open letter (6:5-9), and the attempt at intimidation (6:10-14)? How did each of these ruses build upon the preceding attempts to stop the work on the wall?

3. In keeping with some business people today, Sanballat and his associates had a "hidden agenda." Their letters (Nehemiah 6:1-4) aimed at drawing Nehemiah away from the city in order to harm him. They knew that without his leadership those in Jerusalem would easily fall prey to their machinations. Their open letter (6:5-9) sought to demoralize the Jews by slandering Nehemiah's motives so that it would be harder for Nehemiah to inspire the Jews if another crisis developed. The attempt at intimidation (6:10-14) was really a maneuver to denounce Nehemiah, a God-fearing man, for disobeying the law of the Lord (see Numbers 18:7). From your experience and observation, describe some modern counterparts of these strategies.

   As a leader, Nehemiah was proactive. He determined what he would do. What is the difference between being available to help (as in Nehemiah 5) and being a "puppet of the people"? What was Nehemiah's attitude toward his enemies in each of these incidents in Nehemiah 6?

Something to think about: Nehemiah's ability to handle different difficult situations effectively reminds me of Richard J. Wytmar's statement about the mature executive:

> Executive maturity is not solely a function of chronological age. It is the attainment of a realistic pattern of personal attributes which allow the executive to function with maximum confidence, effectiveness, and accomplishment.

Maturity is that individual state of mind which enables the executive to profit from the experiences of the past in order to resolve the problems of the present and plan for the goals of the future. It is the purposeful division of time, energy, and thought that puts into practical perspective the demands of business and the vital and necessary relationship to family and outside pursuits. It is a continuing and evolving process which adjusts the total needs of the executive to the changing conditions of his existence.

10

MISSION ACCOMPLISHED

Nehemiah 6:10-19

Some Christians have the idea that if they live for the Lord and do what is right He will screen them from all adversity. They attribute trials or testings to some sin they may have committed and, as a result, spend their lives laboring under feelings of guilt and unworthiness.

If Nehemiah had been of this persuasion he might have been tempted to think that after sacrificing the comfort and security of his position at the court of Artaxerxes, the least the Lord could do was bless him with a peaceful governorship. Instead, he faced opposition—from within as well as from without.

In Nehemiah's own recounting of the difficulties he encountered there was, first of all, *intrigue.*

We have all met those who, in their efforts to hinder what we are doing, have reasons for wanting to discuss their differences with us. In reality, all they hope to do is place us on the defensive. They can then claim that we have misjudged them and their intentions. The only safe guide when facing such a seemingly plausible ruse is a clear understanding of where our duty lies. There are, of course, times when a frank discussion of a problem is most important. There are other times, however, when the need of the hour is loyalty to our employers or adherence to our principles. Then there are those occasions when we must insist upon our priorities. This is what Nehemiah did. He discerned the guile of those in Samaria and replied, "I am doing a great work. . . . Why should the work stop while I leave it and dialog with you?"

Having been repulsed, Nehemiah's enemies try a new strategy—indirect derogatory insinuation. Their *innuendo* is a logical sequel to their intrigue. They call in question Nehemiah's motives. This is a very powerful form of attack. It takes advantage of the depravity of human nature. They ask in effect, "What is he getting out of it? He's not doing all this for nothing! There's a personal angle to it somewhere." Nehemiah's altruism is made the subject of biased interpretation.

This kind of attack is not unique. It was the basis of Satan's slander of Job (Job 1:9). The patriotic Jeremiah faced it when he was accused of being in collaboration with the enemy (Jeremiah 37:13). Even the Lord Jesus was falsely arraigned on charges of perverting the nation and stirring up the people (Luke 23:2,5).

But what is to be our response to such slander? Are we to sit back while others misrepresent us and malign our motives?

The appropriate response is one of open denial *and* prayer. In following Nehemiah's example we should deny what is plainly false, refrain from trying to justify our actions, and commit ourselves afresh to the One who judges righteously (see Jeremiah 11:20; 1 Peter 2:23). He is the One before whom every thought and deed will be made manifest (see Luke 12:2; Acts 17:31; Romans 2:5-6,16; 1 Corinthians 3:13; 4:5; etc.). This is what David did when he was vilified by his enemies (Psalm 31:13-15). The Lord Jesus did the same (1 Peter 2:21-23). Such conduct is based on sound psychological principles. It causes us to look away from ourselves to the One on whom we can rely for help. It involves giving Him the sovereignty over our lives. It prevents us from allowing resentment to build up inside; and, by surrendering everything to the Lord, we are kept from harboring thoughts of revenge (Romans 12:19).

Darkening Shadows

As we compare Nehemiah's experience with our own, we see how he was able to cope with the forces which were threatening to undermine his authority. He responded to *intrigue* with manly firmness, and met *innuendo* with open denial and prayer.

And now, as we focus our attention on a more overt form of attack; namely, *intimidation*, we will observe how his actions highlight the need for, and the importance of integrity. Nehemiah, of course, was a man of strong Biblical principles. His life was governed by the Book. Its precepts regulated his conduct and formed an inward standard, which brought all else into conformity to the truth.

The importance of strong spiritual convictions has been underscored by Bernard L. Montgomery, former chief of Imperial General Staff of the British Armed Forces. In his excellent book, *The Path to Leadership*, Viscount Montgomery says, "I firmly believe that in all branches of life in a western democracy, with our long Christian tradition, a leader will not appeal to many unless he possesses Christian virtues." Montgomery defines these virtues as *prudence, justice, temperance, and fortitude.*[1] Without these, no one can withstand the tests of life.

As Christians we live in two worlds. As with Nehemiah, we are surrounded by a pagan environment. We may, however, enjoy his resources. We can follow the teaching of the Scriptures and allow the Word of God to produce in us the truth and character, commitment to principle, and basic adherence to right conduct that is so essential if we are to be successful. The very suddenness with which we sometimes find ourselves in a delicate, trying situation prevents us from planning ahead. We have nothing to guide us, apart from our integrity.[2]

Let's see how all of this may be worked out in practice.

Spy in the Closet

As the entire building operation nears completion, Nehemiah

[1] Prudence, Montgomery claims, is "the habit of referring all matters to divine guidance. On this virtue will hinge wisdom, impartiality, and tact." *Justice*, he says, embodies "the habit of giving to everyone, including God and man himself, their due. On this will hinge the duties of religion, obedience, and gratitude—also integrity, and good will toward others." *Temperance*, which is so necessary in all forms of leadership, includes "self-control, for the highest development of man's nature, and also for personal and social ends. On this hinges purity, humility, and patience." Finally, *fortitude* he describes as "the spirit which resists, endures, and triumphs over the trials and temptations of life. On this will hinge moral courage, industry, and self-discipline." See *The Path to Leadership*, p.13.

[2] I believe that no system of ethics, however well meant or well founded, can long withstand pressures from without unless it is shaped and molded by the Word of God.

learns that one of the priests, a man named Shemiah, is anxious to see him. Shemiah, however, is unable to come to Nehemiah. The text says that he is "shut up" (i.e., confined to his house), but gives us no further explanation.

When Nehemiah visits Shemiah, he is told, as if by a spirit of prophecy,[3] that his enemies have arranged for him to be assassinated. "Come," says Shemiah, "let us meet together in the house of God, within the temple, and let us close the doors of the temple, for they are coming to kill you at night."

Shemiah's proposal is of pagan origin. The area surrounding the temples of antiquity was frequently the refuge of those guilty of all sorts of crimes. Within the temple precincts all were safe. The Temple to which Shemiah refers, however, is not a pagan edifice. It is the sanctuary of the Lord of glory. In making his suggestion to Nehemiah, Shemiah relies upon his new "revelation" to quiet any misgivings the governor may have. Should Nehemiah hesitate at going into the Temple, Shemiah can assure him of immunity from penalty under the Law.

It is important for us to notice that when Shemiah says, "Let us meet together in the house of God, within the *temple*" he uses a term which refers to the Holy Place—a place which only the priests are permitted to enter.

The purpose behind this intimidation is to lead Nehemiah into a compromising situation. If he yields to this supposedly friendly overture, his enemies will expose his fear and use his cowardice to undermine his influence. They will also discount his religious beliefs and point to his flagrant disregard of the Law. Such conduct will immediately discredit him in the eyes of the Jews.

Nehemiah, however, is neither blinded by self-interest, nor overawed by supposed prophetic authority. He has a proper fear-Object (i.e., the Lord), and by walking in submission to His authority, he is kept from stumbling. Had Nehemiah capitulated to Shemiah's blandishments, he would have suc-

[3] Compare Nehemiah 10:8; 12:42. Shemiah must have been prominent in the community and have had Nehemiah's confidence. A lesser man would not have been chosen for the task of intimidating the governor. Shemiah apparently claimed to be a prophet. This would not be the first time a priest, pretending to have the gift of prophecy, had sold himself to the enemy and lied for the sake of monetary gain (see 1 Kings 22:22).

cumbed to an improper fear-object (i.e., Tobiah and the threat of assassination), and the result would have been weakness and timidity.

The Test of a Prophet

Nehemiah's blunt reply: "Should a man like me flee? And could one such as I [a layman] go into the temple and live?[4] I will not go in!" is the best answer to such sophistry. It shows his knowledge of the Word, and the extent to which his *integrity* [5] keeps him from making mistakes. He knows that God is the author of truth. Truth is the essence of His character. God cannot contradict Himself. Seeing that Shemiah's proposal is not in harmony with the plain teaching of God's Word, the prophet must be wrong (see Deuteronomy 13:1-5; 18:20)! Once again Nehemiah's discernment is in evidence. Further conversation with Shemiah confirms his suspicions. God has not sent him. Instead, he has uttered this supposed "prophecy" because he has been hired by Tobiah. The wrongness of his plan and its violation of Biblical principles not only discredits him as a messenger of God, it also exposes the whole scheme concocted by the conspirators in Samaria (Nehemiah 6:13).

Nehemiah is preserved, not by breaking God's Law to escape assassination, but by keeping it!

Nehemiah's encounter with Shemiah, however, leaves him with a deep sense of his own need. He is acutely conscious of the power and subtlety of the opposition. Once again he has recourse to prayer. "Remember, O my God, Tobiah and Sanballat according to these works of theirs, and also Noadiah the prophetess and the rest of the prophets who are trying to frighten me."

Once more Tobiah and those who are with him fail. They have again misjudged Nehemiah. They have made the mistake of evaluating him on the basis of their own standards. All along they have minimized the importance of his practical, working faith!

[4] I.e., "to save his life."

[5] Compare Psalm 15:1-5; 26:1-3; 28:7; Proverbs 11:3,5; Isaiah 33:15-16; Ezekiel 18:5-9.

The Finished Task

In spite of the opposition, the wall is finished in fifty-two days—a remarkable accomplishment for a task regarded as well-nigh impossible.[6] When those who have opposed the work hear of Nehemiah's success, "they lose their confidence, for they perceive that the work has been done with the help of God." Even with such irrefutable evidence of divine approval on Nehemiah's work, there still are enemies within the city as well as without it. They continue to oppose Nehemiah. Tobiah, the Ammonite, has relatives in Jerusalem. He has married a Jewess, the daughter of Shecaniah (see Deuteronomy 23:4), and his son has followed his example by marrying the daughter of Meshullam (Nehemiah 6:18; see also 13:7-8). Correspondence passes between the nobles of Judah and Tobiah. Tobiah's good deeds are paraded before Nehemiah, and Nehemiah's activities are passed on to Tobiah. The threats and innuendos continue as Tobiah tries to weaken Nehemiah's control.

The fact that this chapter closes with a brief statement regarding the continued opposition adds a note of realism to Nehemiah's experience. And so, after all that Nehemiah has done, his trust must still be in the Lord. From the circumstances that Nehemiah faced we learn that even when we have successfully countered all the opposition, watchfulness and prayer must continue to characterize our lives.

By concluding this section with the continued opposition of Tobiah, Nehemiah tends to draw our attention away from his unique accomplishments. This may cause us to miss the important teaching of this passage on the reason for his success. His success may be attributed to three things: his *character*, his *confidence*, and his *courage*.

The Three C's

In working toward his goal, Nehemiah faced obstacles that

[6] It is of interest to note that Nehemiah never claims more than actually took place. In 6:1, his enemies were speaking of the wall as having been completed. Nehemiah, however, knew that the gates had not been hung. In his reckoning the task had not yet been completed. Only when everything has been finished does he record the successful culmination of the work (6:15).

would have caused a man of lesser ability to give up. The most disheartening attacks were directed against his person. Nehemiah withstood them because of *what* (not who) he was. His life proves the truth of the observation that "a man has not more character than he can command in a crisis." His character came directly from his practice of godliness and his close communion with the Lord. Either of these without the other would not have produced the quality of manhood needed if he was successfully to face opposition from implacable foes. What Nehemiah was before God provided the personal dynamic that inspired a downtrodden people to undertake a seemingly impossible task. This same quality of character also helped him persevere against seemingly insurmountable odds.

Nehemiah's character may be traceable directly to his willingness to live under the authority of the Scriptures. His knowledge of the Word equipped him with discernment, and this discernment prevented him from being deceived by those who pretended to be his friends.

We lose our character and our ability to discern the issues which confront us when we neglect the study of the Scriptures. When this happens we find it easy to sacrifice our high ideals of righteousness and integrity on the altars of expediency and selfishness. Real character is a positive thing. It is not the protection of innocence, but the practice of virtue. This forms the basis of effective leadership.

Secondly, there was Nehemiah's confidence. As the obstacles were faced one by one, they gave way before the might of a superior purpose. As Nehemiah faced these seeming impossibilities, they crumbled before his persistence. He succeeded in building the wall of a city and restoring the national dignity of a despised people because he had an unshakable conviction that what he was doing was what God wanted done. His confidence in the Lord released him from the pressure of being "a success," preserved his objectivity, overcame the fears that others endeavored to instill in him, and insured that he was free from undue concern (see Matthew 6:25-34). His confidence enabled him to rise above the storms of adversity, cope with problems, and inspire others to give of their best.

A man's character is the inner dynamic that results in confidence. This confidence is contagious. Without it there can be no effective leadership. These important qualities are, however, insufficient without courage. Courage serves as a powerful antidote to discouragement. It keeps us moving forward when all seems lost.

Nehemiah faced opposition within Jerusalem as well as without. The pressures of those who tried to weaken his resolve and cause him to relinquish his goal were steady and persistent. They knew that *fear* would hinder the implementation of solutions, bring on mediocrity, dull Nehemiah's creativity, and pave the way for his eventual failure. This is where Nehemiah's courage came in. His relationship with the Lord was such that he did not fear what others might think of him or do to him. This does not mean that he ignored the opposition, was careless about his personal safety, or gave way to a *Que sera sera* attitude. His was the faith that moves mountains. His confidence in God gave him the courage to plod on in spite of the clouds of opposition that gathered around him. He boldly championed the cause of right and scorned the things that would inspire fear. Nehemiah's courage helped him attain new heights of achievement. Armed with this fortitude, he turned obstacles into opportunities, and outward trials into personal triumphs.

The foundation for success is laid in our personal character. It is furthered by our confidence in God. This confidence in the Lord and His plan for our lives gives us confidence in ourselves. Finally, what we are, and what we are involved in, is demonstrated by our courage.

1. Success requires certain characteristics of leadership and the development of certain skills. In reviewing Nehemiah's work since he first arrived in Jerusalem (Nehemiah 2:11–6:19), make a list of these skills. Which of these characteristics do you believe to be true of you at the present? What plans can you realistically begin to implement now so as either to improve on or develop the others?

2. In considering Nehemiah 6:10-14, how may you develop a pattern of living that will equip you to discern and withstand false counsel?

3. The pressure to live up to someone else's standards of attainment (i.e., your parents', your boss's, or your own) can prove disheartening. How may a God-given confidence that you are doing what He wants done release you from humanly imposed standards of success?

4. How would you define courage? Does your definition compare favorably or unfavorably with the courage demonstrated by Nehemiah? What differences do you find? How do you account for these differences?

Something to think about: John Adam, Jr., wrote in the *Harvard Business Review*:

> To a very large extent the degree of our business success will depend on our ability to help our people unleash their potential resources by giving them the opportunity to find personal meaning in their work, to expand their personal potential through work, [and] to grow as a result of a sense of accomplishment.

11

"GOD, GIVE US MEN!"

Nehemiah 7:1-73a

Leaders know the importance of setting realistic goals. Without clearly defined objectives it is impossible to build a team's *esprit de corps*. In establishing attainable goals provision should be made for evaluating progress and for anticipating the next major objective.

Nehemiah's first objective was the building of the wall of the city. He motivated the people to work with him and, at different times, measured their advancement (Nehemiah 4:6; 6:1,15). He allowed for interruptions (4:10,13; 5:1-13). Finally the wall was finished; his first objective had been reached. Before the rebuilding of the wall was completed, he took inventory of the situation. His enemies were harassing him, but this did not prevent him from planning ahead. "Phase Two" of the operation, the *consolidation of the work* (see Nehemiah 7 and 11), had already taken shape in his mind.

The importance of advance planning has received considerable attention in recent years. Raymond Brady, editor of *Dun's Review*, observes, "It never pays in business to get so bogged down in the problems of the present that you lose sight of the future—either its opportunities or its pitfalls." Proper planning concerns all of us, whether we work in commerce or industry, the church or missions, education or politics. Nehemiah's advance planning illustrates the ways we may make adequate preparation for the future.

Search for the Solution

As we examine Nehemiah's plans for consolidation we begin with an analysis of chapter 7. Here again we have a long list of names. These names make this chapter even more difficult to handle than Nehemiah 3. There the text was made easy to interpret due to the occurrence of repetitious phrases. No such help can be gleaned from the text this time. How then are we to explain it?

In one of his lectures at Dallas Seminary, Dr. Howard Hendricks said: "Whenever you are faced with a problem in interpretation, climb a 'contextual tree.' "

When I heard this, it brought to mind the experience of a friend of mine in Canada, who was a member of our church. He was serving as a captain with the Royal Canadian Mounted Police. His experience in wilderness survival had been so thorough that he was commissioned by his superiors to train the rookies.

As is true of many Canadians, our friend liked hunting. On one of his trips, he found himself on a level plain with no mountains or other landmarks to break the horizon. In a ravine close to his camp, he saw the spoor of some elk. He followed the tracks down the gorge, up one side and through some dense thickets. These thickets were interspersed throughout the plain. The trail was a long one—much longer than he had at first supposed—and with the sun declining rapidly in the west, he experienced an inward twinge of fear. This happened even before his mental faculties admitted that he was lost. The terrain made it impossible for him to sight any promontories. His only "landmark" was the ravine, and it was hidden by the numerous stands of thick trees through which he had passed.

Finally, finding a tall tree on the edge of one of the thickets, he climbed it and began looking for the ravine. The shadows were lengthening and already there was a cold nip in the air. It was a sure sign of frost that night.

Much to my friend's surprise, the ravine, when he finally spotted it, was not to the right as he had expected, but behind him. Once he located it, it was just a matter of time before he was back at camp.

Only those who have engaged in wilderness camping know how easy it is to become lost. In much the same way, only those who have tried to explain difficult portions of the Scriptures know how readily they can lose sight of the central purpose of the book and become lost in the minutia.

In tackling chapter 7, we will follow Professor Hendricks' recommendation and climb a "contextual tree." From this vantage point we will be able to look back over the chapters we have covered and forward to the chapters ahead. This will tell us exactly *where* we are and explain *why* God saw fit to include this particular chapter in His Word.

Chapters 1—6 show us how Nehemiah accomplished his first objective—the building of the wall. *Chapter seven is transitional and records the first steps toward consolidating the work.* This move towards consolidation will soon be interrupted by a spiritual awakening (chapters 8—10), but will resume again after God has prepared the heart of His people for self-government (chapter 11).

The first thing we notice as we look into this chapter is the new leadership Nehemiah provides for the city (Nehemiah 7:1-4). Following this, God prompts him to take a census of the people. This is done with a view to determining the purity of the people and the priesthood, and in anticipation of the repopulation of Jerusalem (7:5-69). Finally, Nehemiah insures the proper support of those engaged in the service of the house of the Lord (7:70-73a).

The result of Nehemiah's own advance planning and God's prompting is a big step toward the revival of national prestige and an inward yearning on the part of the people to know more of God's will for their lives.

Leaders Are Made

As Nehemiah initiates "Phase Two," he selects reliable men to whom he can delegate certain responsibilities. "Now it came about that when the wall was rebuilt . . . that I put Hanani my brother, and Hananiah the commander of the fortress, in charge of Jerusalem, for he was a faithful man and feared God more than many."

But what leadership qualifications did these men possess? Wasn't Nehemiah guilty of nepotism in assigning to his own brother the administration of the city?

Nehemiah's actions need to be viewed in the light of his position and commission. In appointing new leadership over the city, he exemplifies what Alexander Hamilton later put into words: "The aim of every political constitution is, or ought to be, first to obtain for rulers men who possess most wisdom to discern, and most virtue to pursue the common good of society; and in the next place, to take the most effectual precautions for keeping them virtuous."

In Hanani, Nehemiah sees a man who is concerned for others. Having been reared in the same home, Nehemiah knows that Hanani has received the same basic training he was privileged to receive. Whereas Nehemiah entered the king's service and became a courtier, Hanani's patriotism caused him to leave the land of his birth and return (perhaps with Ezra) to Jerusalem. When the plight of the Jews became such that they felt it necessary to petition the king, Hanani was commissioned to go unheralded and unannounced to Babylon and intercede on their behalf. This reveals not only his courage (see Esther 4:16b) but also the confidence his countrymen have in him. Possessed of these qualities, Nehemiah does not hesitate to place him in a position of rulership over the city.

And Hananiah is made commander over the fortress. His faithfulness to the Lord and loyalty to His Word will be sorely needed with traitorous Jews in high places and leading families involved in intrigue. Nehemiah knows from his years at court that when a *coup* is attempted it is invariably accomplished with the might of the army backing the rebels. For this reason it is imperative that he have a godly man in this important position.

In Nehemiah's actions we see once again his astute handling of a potentially difficult situation. While placing a member of his own family over the city of Jerusalem may, at first sight, appear to be an act of nepotism, the fact remains that Hanani is highly qualified for the position and, being probably of royal blood, will immediately command the respect of the nationalistic citizens within the city.

Some, however, will still question the wisdom of such a move. After all, they may reason, what will be Artaxerxes' reaction when he finds a descendant of King David occupying such an important position?

A study of Artaxerxes' administration reveals that as long

as an appointee exercised his responsibilities under a governor or satrap, and remained loyal to the crown, there would be no opposition to his appointment from the Persian court. Artaxerxes practiced what Theodore Roosevelt later recommended when he said, "The best executive is the one who has sense enough to pick good men to do what he wants done, and self-restraint enough to keep from meddling with them while they do it."

Having carefully selected the new leaders of the city, Nehemiah illustrates a second principle of sound administrative practice, namely the proper development of one's subordinates. Having already insured that the gatekeepers and singers, and the rest of the Levites[1] will act as watchmen on the wall during daylight hours, he gives Hanani and Hananiah general guidelines for safeguarding the city (Nehemiah 7:3-4). The Levites will supervise the opening and closing of the gates, but at night the citizens themselves will be responsible for guarding the wall. Under the new leadership, the people will once more be called on to stand watch "each at his post, and each in front of his own house."

The safeguarding of the city brings to the fore another matter. The city is spacious and there are relatively few residents. The need for urban renewal, therefore, becomes obvious. God prompts Nehemiah to take a census of the people. While a program for repopulating the city will not be instituted immediately, due to a spiritual renewal which is about to take place, the preparation undertaken now will prepare the way for its future implementation (see Nehemiah 11).

Guardians of the Soul

While taking the census, Nehemiah finds a record of the Jews who had returned to their homeland under Zerubbabel

[1] The gatekeepers and singers were Levites (Ezra 2:40-42,70; 7:24; 10:23-24; Nehemiah 7:43-45,73; 10:28; etc.). The priests and Levites formed half the population of Jerusalem (see Nehemiah 11:6-19; 1 Chronicles 9:9-22). The responsibility for guarding the temple area had traditionally been a task allotted them (1 Chronicles 9:17-22; 26:12-19).

(538 B.C.; Nehemiah 7:6-69). A similar record is found in Ezra 2.[2] The census prepares the way for the repopulation of the city. This goal is temporarily lost sight of because in verses 61-65 we read of some people who are now dismissed from the priesthood. They have been officiating in the Temple and have worked with the others in building the wall. Now, however, they are regarded as "impure" and removed from office. At some time in the past their forebears had intermarried with Gentiles. As a result, they can no longer prove the purity of their ancestry. There is no alternative but for them to return to their secular pursuits until someone can prove their ancestral claim.

But isn't this harsh treatment for those who have labored long and hard on rebuilding the wall? What purpose can such a high-handed policy serve? This is a time for unity, not for hairsplitting over doctrinal differences.

In much the same way that Nehemiah has instituted new leadership to safeguard the temporal well-being of the citizens of Jerusalem, so now he takes steps to safeguard the spiritual welfare of the people. His seemingly harsh treatment of those who cannot prove their genealogy does not offend Jewish commentators. They are quick to recognize the disobedience of those who had intermarried with the Gentiles and readily concur with Nehemiah in his actions. If the priesthood is corrupt, its influence will ultimately destroy the moral and spiritual fiber of the people. The danger facing the people is too great to be decided on mere sentiment. A pure priesthood is essential if the people are to maintain a right relationship with the Lord.

The teaching of this passage is not without its parallel today. We have men occupying the pulpits of our land who are unable to prove their spiritual birth. They do not know what it is to be saved. To them conversion is an enigma and, by right, they should be excluded from our pulpits. They have become "wedded" to false doctrines, their teaching is corrupt and their lives

---

[2] C. F. Keil in *The Books of Ezra, Nehemiah, and Esther* (n.d.), demonstrates the amazing accuracy of these lists. John J. Davis, in *Biblical Numerology* (1968), has elaborated on the difficulties facing those who try to reconcile these ancient records. The list in Nehemiah 7, while made many years before Nehemiah's appointment as governor, gives evidence of having been compiled *after* the people arrived in "the land beyond the river." It reflects changes which Zerubbabel's list could not.

are a pretense. Only those who have experienced the saving grace of Jesus Christ for themselves and daily put into practice the benefits of His salvation can hope to minister to others. We, therefore, have much to learn from Nehemiah's example.

In further implementing "Phase Two" of his plan, Nehemiah insures that those who work in the Temple will be adequately supported (Nehemiah 7:70-73a). As a consequence of the census, the heads of the fathers' houses are again brought into prominence in the community. They have long been overshadowed by the rulers of the different cities. For years they have been unable to exercise their influence over the people. Now, however, they come to the fore once more and willingly give to the work of the Lord. Nehemiah[3] also makes a large donation, and the temple servants are well provided for. All of this contributes toward the stability of the economy.

Responsibility or Restraint

A brief review of Nehemiah's conduct in this chapter will reinforce several important principles.

First, all key men in business should be engaged in training their subordinates to assume positions of responsibility and leadership. George Olmstead, a retired general of the United States Army, writing in *The Industrial Banker*, pointed out that "if our free enterprise system is to prove its superiority . . . our greatest hope lies in finding and developing young men and women with talents for leadership. Private enterprise can only be as strong as the men and women who run our businesses. Our future survival depends upon the success of our programs of leadership development—not only in business, but also in all areas of our national life. This, then, must be our objective. Our program for leadership development must succeed." The same

---

[3] In this chapter, Nehemiah is referred to as the *Tirshathah*, a Persian title carrying with it the idea of power and dignity and indicating the extent of the governor's domain (see Nehemiah 7:65,70; 8:9). It is evident that these verses were penned by someone else, for when Nehemiah speaks of himself, he uses the term *Pechah* (Nehemiah 5:14; etc.). The fact that someone else (possibly Malachi) wrote these verses (and chapters 8—10) does not mean that they are uninspired or of less value. The Holy Spirit superintended their composition and guided Nehemiah in the inclusion of them in his "Memoirs."

principle holds true in our churches and on the mission field as well (see 2 Timothy 2:2).

In appointing men to positions of leadership, we should provide them with the necessary guidelines, delegate adequate responsibility to them, and allow them to "carry the ball." Hopefully those whom we entrust with administrative tasks will, as with Hanani and Hananiah, be able to build on our strengths and thereby make their own weaknesses irrelevant. Only by cultivating leaders can our churches and missionary societies, businesses and educational institutions break out of the mold of being passive response systems and adapt to the demands of the present. Only then can they become a dynamic, creative force with a vision for the future. The need, therefore, is for leaders who will give people the opportunity to explore their own potentialities by striving to create new possibilities for themselves and others.

Secondly, there is the need for Christian leaders to be open to direction from the Lord. We need to have our senses tuned to His prompting (see Nehemiah 7:5). The great men of the ages have realized the importance of seeking God's guidance, not only in the big things of life, but in the little ones as well. George Washington Carver was one of these. On one occasion he remarked: "There is no need for anyone to be without direction in the midst of the perplexities of this life. Are we not plainly told, 'In all thy ways acknowledge Him, and He will direct thy path'?" It was Dr. Carver's custom to arise at 4:00 A.M. each day and seek God's guidance for his life. In speaking of this habit, he said, "At no other time have I so sharp an understanding of what God means to do with me as in those hours when other folks are still asleep." In this seemingly simple practice we have the secret of his phenomenal success.

Next, there is the importance of adequate spiritual leadership. Disobedience and adherence to faulty doctrine (with its subsequent undermining of moral principles) is the chief reason for the condition of our present-day society. As is always the case, spiritual laxity begins in our seminaries and then spreads to our pulpits. It begins with those who pay little more than "lip service" to Christ as the Head of His Church, compromise on important doctrines like the authority of the Word, and fail systematically to teach the Scriptures to those who sit under their ministry. What we need today is men in our seminaries and in our pulpits who are thoroughly grounded in Bible and theology, who will faithfully declare "the whole counsel of God" (Acts 20:27). The greatest danger comes from those who are syncretistic in their beliefs and are no longer capable of expounding the Bible with power and insight. They should be put out of the ministry, regardless of whether they be teachers or preachers.

Finally, from Nehemiah's example we see the need adequately to support the work of the Lord. Many good evangelical men of God serving in pastorates and on the mission fields, and many fine God-honoring institutions, suffer continued economic hardship because believers do not adequately maintain His work. Now, more than ever before, believers need to stand behind Christian organizations and, by means of their gifts, advance the cause of Christ.

1. In what specific ways did Nehemiah begin to consolidate the gains of the past eight weeks (Nehemiah 7:1-4)? How did he implement his plan? Whom did Nehemiah appoint to positions of leadership? How did Nehemiah's actions take care of the criticism of 6:6?

2. What qualities did the new leaders, Hanai and Hananiah, possess? Was there wisdom in Nehemiah's choice? Why? What may we learn about delegating from Nehemiah 7? What are we doing to train those under us for increased leadership responsibilities?

3. What events led up to the census (Nehemiah 7:5-69)? Why was it necessary? What did Nehemiah hope to achieve by or do with the results of this enrollment? Why was Nehemiah so hard on certain of the priests (7:61-65)? Is purity on the part of those who minister to us in the name of the Lord important? Why was the purity of the priests important to the ancient Jews?

4. Why is it important for us to support those who minister to us? What does the New Testament teach (see Luke 10:7; 1 Timothy 5:17; etc.)? How would you go about fixing a pastor's salary?

Something to think about: A. W. Tozer in *The Next Chapter After the Last*, wrote:

> We are sent to bless the world, but never to compromise with it. Our glory lies in a spiritual withdrawal from that [which] builds on dust.

RECHARGING ONE'S BATTERIES

Nehemiah 7:73b—8:18

A few years ago, an article entitled "The Scandal of Biblical Illiteracy" startled the readers of *Christianity Today*. The writer, Dr. Richard Lyon Morgan, gave the results of a test given freshmen entering a church-related college. The questions asked were elementary ones such as, "Where was Jesus born?" "Which was the earliest of the four gospels?" "Name some of Paul's letters," etc. The average grade scored by these students was 10 per cent, with the highest being 34 per cent.

"The results [of this test]," said Dr. Morgan, "in no sense reflect the intellectual abilities of these students, for all of them had survived the many hurdles that would have kept the unqualified from entering college. *But the results do point to a real crisis in the teaching of the Bible in church and home.* And this Biblical illiteracy is not restricted to college students. . . . Despite all the outward signs . . . there exists a 'famine for hearing the Word of God.' "[1]

Many people—Christian people—fail to understand the place and importance of the Bible in their daily lives. They are spiritually ignorant of God's provision for them. But how can a knowledge of the Bible make a difference in a person's life? What steps may a person take to transform the neglect of a lifetime?

True spiritual renewal comes only when individuals turn from their religious languor and moral apathy to God in repentance and faith. It involves submission to the authority of the Scriptures. How all this may become a part of our experience is illustrated for us in Nehemiah 8.

[1] *Christianity Today* (1965), p. 817. Used by permission.

The Problem of Freedom

With the wall of the city built and the first steps toward consolidation under way, God interrupts the work. The people are not ready for self-government. If they are allowed to continue in the course they are taking, they will ultimately fail. Traitors are within the city. Intrigue is rife. And there is a need for a solid foundation to be laid if they are to build for the future.[2] They need a spiritual renewal which will establish a sense of community, or *koinonia*, among them.

Daniel Webster stressed the importance of a proper foundation on which to establish a new society. Having observed the trend of history he pointed out that "there is no solid basis for civilization but in the Word of God. If we abide by the principles taught in the Bible, our country will go on prospering.... The Bible is a book . . . which teaches man his own individual responsibility, his own dignity, and his equality with his fellowman."

The Israelites need to be right with God if they are to prosper as a nation. Their interest in spiritual realities leads them to ask Ezra to read the law to them. Their desire stems from three seemingly unrelated things: the persistent teaching ministry of Ezra (Ezra 7:10); the inspiring example of Nehemiah; and a new awareness of the righteousness required by God. This awareness may well have come about when those who could not prove their genealogy were thrust out of the priesthood (Nehemiah 7:61-65). As a consequence, when the seventh month (Tisri)[3] comes, the sons of Israel leave their cities and journey to Jerusalem. There they "gather as one man at the

[2] There is an interesting parallel to these events in the early history of the United States. The importance of the Word of God in the lives of the people was boldly affirmed by Thomas Jefferson. He said, "The Bible is the cornerstone of liberty." Andrew Jackson claimed, "The Bible is the rock on which our Republic rests." The importance of sound Biblical principles for the establishment of any system of government has been underscored by A. Mervyn Davis in *Foundation of American Freedom* (1955).

[3] Two feasts and one fast were held in Jerusalem during the month Tisri. On the first day of the month there was the feast of trumpets (Leviticus 23:23-25; Numbers 29:1-6). Ten days later this feast was followed by a fast—the Day of Atonement (Leviticus 16:29ff; 23:7; 25:9). After this came the week-long feast of tabernacles (Leviticus 23:24,39,41).

square which is in front of the water gate, and they ask Ezra the scribe to bring the book of the law of Moses, which the LORD had given to Israel" and to read to them from it. In this act, they show their spiritual hunger for the Word of God.

The Pursuit of Freedom

As they assemble before the water gate, Ezra mounts a podium made especially for the occasion (see Leviticus 23:24; Deuteronomy 31:10-13). He is accompanied by thirteen priests.[4] Before he reads the Law, he leads them in prayer. He invokes God's blessing on those present, and they respond by saying, " 'Amen (so be it!) Amen!' while lifting up their hands; then they bow low and worship the LORD with their faces to the ground."

In these actions we catch a glimpse of the desire of their hearts. They are conscious of their need and readily join with Ezra in praying for the Lord to be gracious to them. During Ezra's prayer, the whole congregation stands with their arms lifted above their heads and their palms turned heavenward. This has traditionally been the Jewish way of saying, "Lord, I am empty handed. I have nothing. Everything that I need comes from You."

By leading the people in prayer, Ezra prepares the hearts of the people for what is to follow. He arouses their anticipation by reminding them of the faithfulness of their covenant-keeping God. As they bow and worship before the Lord they intimate by their actions their submission to His authority.

When the prayer is over Ezra unrolls the scroll and reads from the Law to "the men, women, and all who are able to listen with understanding." Other religions regarded women

---

[4] Among the priests is one named Urijah (Nehemiah 8:4; see 3:4,21). Urijah is also mentioned in Ezra 8:33. The occurrence of his name in both books is of historic significance. A certain school of Bible critics has long held that the book of Ezra *follows* Nehemiah and is to be dated around 398 B. C. The interesting point in connection with Urijah is that he was a father and active in the time of Nehemiah, and it is most unlikely that he would have retained his vigor to the supposed time of Ezra's arrival in Jerusalem if this had indeed occurred 50 years later. It is preferable to date the arrival of Ezra in Jerusalem at 458 B. C., thirteen years *before* the time of Nehemiah. As is so often the case, the Bible's own chronology is more reliable and more consistent than the superimposed chronology of its critics.

and children as nonentities. Only in Judaism and Christianity are they treated with dignity and respect.

There are many Bible students who believe that Ezra read from the book of Deuteronomy. The reaction of the people fits its context. Ezra may, however, have read selections from all the Torah (i.e., the first five books of the Bible).[5] He reads the Word distinctly and the Levites explain the text to the people.[6] The words of the Law are understood by all who hear it and their response shows its effect on their *minds*, their *emotions*, and their *wills*.

In this connection, there is a parallel between Ezra's time and our own. Today the church languishes as a result of the failure of its appointed ministers to teach the Word (2 Timothy 4:2). When C. H. Spurgeon came to London he found that the people "were so starved, that a morsel of the gospel was a treat to them." He began *expounding* the Scriptures. A remarkable work for the Lord took place. People were saved week by week without the need of an evangelist. Years later, when Spurgeon died, it was said that the people in his congregation knew more of their Bibles than the theologians. The key to Spurgeon's success lay in his exposition of the Word of God. He taught it; the people heard it and applied it to their lives (James 1:21-25), and the result was a continuous movement of the Spirit in their midst.

The Privileges of Freedom

The spiritual renewal of the people of Judah begins with a challenge to the mind (Nehemiah 8:1-8). It continues in the effect it has on their emotions (8:9-12). Having come under the

[5] Compare Nehemiah 10:30 and Exodus 34:16; Nehemiah 10:31 and Leviticus 25:2-7; Nehemiah 10:35-39 and Leviticus 27:30; Numbers 15:20-21; 18:11-32.

[6] "And the ears of all the people are to the word" is a literal rendering of the Hebrew text. The Law which Ezra reads had been written in Hebrew, while the people speak Aramaic. To be sure there is a great similarity between these two Semitic languages. Some of the people, however, may never have mastered Hebrew. Ezra, therefore, has Levites stationed at strategic places to "explain the law to the people." This takes the form of translating what Ezra is reading and explaining (i.e., expounding) its meaning. The fact that people stand "in their places" indicates that they are divided into groups. This makes the teaching of the Word much easier.

teaching of the Law, the people now compare their conduct with the standard set forth in the Word. They become conscious of their sin. They see how far short of God's standard they have fallen (see Psalm 119:130; Romans 3:20). Conviction is borne in their hearts and their contrition is expressed in weeping before the Lord.

THE BASIS OF SPIRITUAL RENEWAL

		READING OF THE WORD, Nehemiah 7:73b—8:8a		
INTELLECT	APPEAL TO THE MIND	Hunger for the Word	Method Adopted	Time
	Request of the People	All the people gathered Ezra requested to read the Law Men and women stood Leaders led by example	Scribes stood Expounded distinctly Gave the sense Caused the people to understand	7th Month First Day 7:73a—8:8a
	Ministry of Ezra	Propagation of the Word	The Time	
		Gathered themselves Stood from morning to midday	1st day of 7th month	First day of the Feast of Weeks
	Challenge to the Mind	Attentive All stood—unity of purpose Lifted up their hands	Early morning until midday	
			The Place	
	Response of the Mind	Retention of the Word	Broad place (outside the Temple)	
		Heard with understanding	At the Water Gate	
		EXPLANATION OF THE WORD, Nehemiah 8:8b		
SENSIBILITIES	EFFECT ON THE EMOTIONS	EXHORTATION FROM THE WORD, Nehemiah 8:9-12		
	Result of Conviction	Response to the Word		
		Natural reaction 8:9 Emotions (Guilt)—weeping		
	Change of Disposition	Proper reaction 8:10 Joy		
		Result: Strength, 8:10		
WILL	CHALLENGE TO THE WILL	OBEDIENCE TO THE WORD, Nehemiah 8:13-18		
	Discovery of the Word	Submission to the Word		
		The pattern for submission, 8:13-15,18		
	Instruction in the Word	The implementation of submission (action) The people gathered and understood, verse 13 They found and published, verse 14		Second Day, 8:13
	Obedience to the Word	They went and gathered, verse 16 They made booths and sat under them, verse 17 They read the Word.		(Total of one week, 8:18)
		Result: THERE WAS VERY GREAT GLADNESS		

The feast days in Israel's worship were intended to be joyous occasions (Deuteronomy 12:7,12,18; 14:26; 16:11,14; Zechariah

8:19). They were designed to bring glory to the Lord. Nehemiah,[7] Ezra, and the Levites remind them of this and instruct them to engage in acts of hospitality (Deuteronomy 16:11,14; 26:12; 1 Samuel 9:13; 2 Samuel 6:19). "Go, eat the fat [Leviticus 2:1-3; 6:21], drink the sweet, and send portions to him who has nothing prepared [Deuteronomy 14:29; 16:10; 26:12]; for this day is holy to the Lord. Do not be grieved, for *the joy of the Lord is your strength.*" In this statement we have the essence of our spiritual experience. It is possible to become too absorbed with our own failures and shortcomings. This is unhealthy. "Man's chief end is to glorify God and to enjoy Him forever." Instead of being introspective and self-centered, we need to become other-directed (James 1:27). When we take an interest in others we begin to experience real joy.

Joy is not an ethereal "something" that is divorced from reality. Joy becomes a vital part of our experience when we rejoice in our standing before God. This takes place as we learn more of what He has done for us and enter into the *reality* of what it means to belong to Him and be accepted by Him. When this happens, we experience joy. From this time onward our work is characterized by self-forgetfulness. We are now able to live for His glory.

The people of Nehemiah's day experience joy because the Lord has again become the center of their lives. They feel secure in their relationship with Him. This gives them a feeling of well-being, protection, care, and freedom from concern. In this security, they become conscious of their worth. With His blessing upon them, they feel competent to face the future. The result is strength (1 Chronicles 16:27), and their natural response is one of obedience to His will. They go their way "to eat, to drink, to send portions, and to celebrate (lit., 'make a great rejoicing') a great festival, *because they understand the words which have been made known to them.*"

The Perpetuation of Freedom

Whereas spiritual renewal begins with a knowledge of the Word and is designed to have an effect on our emotions, it has

---

[7] In chapters 8—10, Nehemiah takes a "back seat" and leaves matters almost entirely in the hands of the priests.

no lasting effect unless it affects our wills. In the concluding paragraph we have described for us the desire of the people to know and to do the will of the Lord (Nehemiah 8:13-18).

On the second day, the heads of the fathers' households gather together and ask Ezra to instruct them further in the law of the Lord.[8] As Ezra reads to them, they find that they have not kept the feast of tabernacles (or booths) during the seventh month. They determine to remedy this oversight. Their decision to keep the feast shows their submission to the authority of the Word of God. [9]

In addition, the desire of the Jews to learn more of the Law is shown by the fact that Ezra is asked to hold *daily* "Bible readings." With such earnestness, it is no wonder that a spirit of renewal becomes evident. And through this experience the people are prepared for self-government.

The experience of the Jews highlights one of the reasons why we need continuously to expose ourselves to the teaching of God's Word. So many new ideas traffic through our minds each day that many vitally important truths are forgotten. When we forget God's absolutes, we lack the discernment we need to face different kinds of situations. By continuously exposing ourselves to the teaching of the Word, we are reminded of the Biblical principles that should govern our lives.

The importance of spiritual principles in the life of any people was affirmed by William McKinley. He pointed out that "the more profoundly we study this wonderful Book [the Bible], and the more closely we observe its divine precepts, the better citizens we will become and the higher will be the destiny of our nation."

[8] The people come to Ezra to be instructed in "the words of the law." They want to *understand* how it relates to their lives. The Hebrew word *l'haskil* means: "to give intelligent consideration to" (see Psalm 101:2; Daniel 9:13). The mind must be enlightened before the will can respond.

[9] The feast of tabernacles looked *back* to the time of the Exodus and reminded the Jews of the wandering of their fathers in the desert. It also looked *forward* to their settlement in the land under the promised Messiah. For a concise summary of the prophetic significance of Israel's feasts, see the author's book, *Searching for Identity* (1975), pp. 48-49. The Jews of Nehemiah's time kept this feast on a larger scale than had been done since the time of Joshua, nearly 1,000 years earlier.

The Basis of Unity

The effect of the Bible upon the people of Israel is not hard to trace. It provides a basis for true unity. The people are united in their desire to learn more of the Word of the Lord. All classes are included. Their unity of purpose not only brings them together, it places them in a position where God can bless them. They join together in showing their respect for the Law; and their obedience brings with it a sense of community. Whereas previously they had not been prepared for self-government because of their disunity, the spirit of renewal begins to heal these divisions. And as the people learn more of God's Law, their national identity is strengthed.[10]

There is a great deal of talk today about the "unity" of the church. Church groups are banding together in the hope that by uniting they will gain strength. The Bible does emphasize the unity of believers, but never of churches or denominations. Furthermore, those who advocate ecumenism establish their basis for unity upon the lowest common denominator—only those beliefs to which all participants can subscribe. The result is the erosion of the authority of God's revelation to man and the discarding of many of the cardinal doctrines of the Christian faith.

In the New Testament, this sense of unity is expressed by the word *koinonia*. It means a spirit of sharing, of fellowship, of oneness. It is a bond that binds believers to each other. This sense of community is based upon a likeness of nature (2 Peter 1:4). It helps us live together in harmony because of a real sense of love for one another (John 13:34ff; 15:12). The practical outworking of this fellowship shows itself in the strong Christian bearing the burdens of the weaker brother (Romans 1:4; 1 Corinthians 8). This oneness is *not* established upon the lowest common denominator (i.e., the minimal points of doctrine upon which all can agree). Instead, Christ is held in honor as Lord and submission is to the authority of God as Father. The unity of faith spoken of in the Bible allows for diversity

[10] The Israelites had long suffered under the oppressing hands of those in Samaria. Even now they are numerically inferior to their enemies. Their need for unity—spiritual and national—is obvious. Horace Greenly pointed out: "It is impossible to mentally or socially enslave a Bible-reading public."

without division, and uniformity without controlled conformity. God's Word becomes our authority and influences our business practices and social conduct. To the extent that we follow the teaching of the Bible, we are able to enjoy God's blessing upon our lives.

The blessings of this kind of fellowship are many. In addition to the personal and corporate fellowship with the Father (1 John 1:3,6) and with the Son (1 Corinthians 1:9), there is also fellowship in Christ's sufferings (Philippians 3:10) and the Holy Spirit, who guides us into all truth (2 Corinthians 13:14; Philippians 2:1), empowers us for every task, and acts as an Umpire in our souls whenever we are faced with decisions and do not know what to do.

How may these blessings be ours? By submitting ourselves entirely to the teaching of the Word of God, and by allowing the Scriptures to permeate our thinking, regulate our emotions, and direct our wills. Only as we put into practice what is taught in the Bible can spiritual, mental, and emotional well-being become a part of our experience. How this is *attained* is explained in Nehemiah 8. The way in which it may be *maintained* is described for us in Nehemiah 9.

1. What, in your estimation, has given rise to the general "Biblical illiteracy" to which Dr. Morgan referred in his article (described on page 139)?

   Of what practical value is submission to the authority of Scripture? To what extent did Ezra live under the authority of God's Word (Ezra 7:10)? How does such a lifestyle prepare one to teach (or "expound") Scripture?

2. Describe in your own words the request the Jews made of Ezra (Nehemiah 8:1). What does this request tell us about their needs? Why was there such hunger of heart? What do 8:13 and 8:18 add to our understanding of the sincerity of their request? Is there a parallel between what Ezra did for the Jews of his time and the ministry of an expository preacher today? If so, what kind of parallel?

3. How may Christians experience a genuine revival? What are its prerequisites? In what ways would this kind of spiritual renewal make a difference in your life? Why, in genuine spiritual renewal, does God involve our minds, our emotions, and our wills?

4. If you were to evaluate the spiritual state of the church at large in our generation, what would you say are its greatest deficiencies? What are its evident strengths? How may its spiritual needs be met?

Something to think about: In 1534, after Martin Luther had translated the Bible into German, the common people turned to it eagerly, buying thousands of copies. Luther's New Testament (which had appeared only a short time before) had gone through seventeen Wittenberg editions by 1533, thirteen from the presses at Augsburg, twelve from Bale, and thirteen from Strasburg. One Catholic prelate lamented:

> Even shoemakers, women, and ignorant people, who have learned only a little German, are eagerly reading [the Bible]

as the fountain of all truth, and that, with such frequency that they know it by heart. They carry it about with them and have attained such knowledge of it that they dispute not only with Catholic laymen but with doctors of theology, about faith and the gospel.

13

THE LESSONS OF HISTORY

Nehemiah 9

As we scan the highways of history, we find them strewn with the wreckage of those nations that forgot God. From the earliest times to the present there is not a single record of any civilization maintaining its moral fiber without an adequate religious foundation. All of this highlights the importance of the spiritual renewal of the Jews in Judah. Without a firm religious commitment they were unfit for self-government.

In Nehemiah 8 we saw how the spirit of renewal began with a hunger for the Word. When the Law was read, it produced conviction in the hearts of those who heard it. The people repented of their sin and submitted themselves to the Lord. Then came the Day of Atonement, and later on, the feast of tabernacles. On the second day after the feast of tabernacles, the Israelites gather together in solemn assembly. Their leaders are anxious to conserve the results of the spiritual awakening which has taken place.

It is not hard for us to understand this move on the part of the leaders. We have all been in situations where we felt the Spirit of God working in our lives. If we failed to take full advantage of this experience then, with the passing of time, our spiritual enthusiasm waned and we reverted back to our original state. Ezra and the Levites were apparently as aware of this human failing as we are. They, therefore, took steps to bring the people to a place of renewed dedication to the Lord. The procedure is described for us in Nehemiah 9 and 10. These chapters form a unit. Chapter 9 recounts the history of the Israelites and provides a fitting prelude to the signing of the covenant in chapter 10.

Chapter 9 is divided into three main parts.

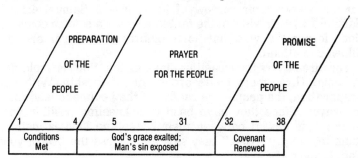

PREPARATION OF THE PEOPLE	PRAYER FOR THE PEOPLE	PROMISE OF THE PEOPLE
1 — 4	5 — 31	32 — 38
Conditions Met	God's grace exalted; Man's sin exposed	Covenant Renewed

The main segment, covering verses 5-31, surveys redemptive program from the time of Adam to the Babylonian captivity. It contains four sections: from creation to Abraham (5-8); from the captivity to the Red Sea (9-15); from the wandering in the desert to possession of the land (16-25); from the judges to captivity (26-31).

The Sense of History

"Now on the twenty-fourth day of this month,[1] the sons of Israel assemble with fasting, in sackcloth, and with dirt upon them. And the descendants of Israel separate themselves from the sons of strangers [i. e., foreigners] and stand and confess their sins, and the iniquities of their fathers. While they remain in their place, Ezra reads from the book of the law of the LORD, their God, for a fourth of the day; and for another fourth they confess and worship the LORD, their God."

As the Israelites gather together before the Lord, they give evidence of their contrition. Their abstinence bears witness to their devotion, while the sackcloth symbolizes their inner

[1] The feast of tabernacles lasted from the 15th to the 22d of Tisri. The special day of penance described in Nehemiah 9 was not scheduled for the 23d of the month (which was left to serve as a transition from joy to sorrow), but was held on the 24th. The feast of tabernacles symbolized the blessing of Israel in the millennium under their Messiah. It was a time of joy. The present condition of the people was a far cry from the anticipation of the events celebrated in the feast. When they met on the 24th Tisri, it was to keep a fast.

repentance, and the scattering of earth or ashes on their heads further shows their sorrow of heart (see 1 Samuel 4:12; 2 Samuel 13:19). In view of the fact that this is a solemn convocation, foreigners who have not embraced Judaism are not allowed to attend.

For three hours the Israelites stand as the Word is explained to them. Three more hours are spent in worship. With this preparation, the people are ready for the Levites to lead them in prayer. Since they have been in a kneeling position with their heads bowed between their knees, the Levites instruct them to stand. "Arise," they say, and "bless the LORD, your God, forever and ever."

This must have been a most impressive sight. The Israelites were numerically inferior to their enemies. Their faith, however, had been quickened by the promises of God. The example they set should encourage evangelical Christians who may be tempted to think of themselves as a weak and relatively ineffective minority. To us, as to the Israelites of old, comes the assurance that prayer is a greater power than any possible combination of man-made powers. It places us in touch with God, and enables us to tap His infinite resources.

The Choice of Life

The Levites begin their prayer with adoration. They contemplate God's majesty, extol His power, and describe His gracious intervention on behalf of His people.

With this as a basis, those present are then led to consider the *example* of Abraham. The Lord had called Abraham from the land of the Chaldeans and had led him to the land of promise. To confirm His word to Abraham, God had made a covenant with him (Genesis 12:1-3; etc.).[2] This covenant prom-

[2] The Abrahamic Covenant promised to Abraham and his descendants a land, Canaan; a seed, Isaac, through whom the Messiah would come; and personal, national, and universal blessing. Abraham died without having received all that God promised him (Hebrews 11:39-40). In the millennium, however, following the resurrection of the righteous dead (Daniel 12:2-3), he and the other Old Testament saints will receive the complete fulfillment of all God pledged Himself to give them.

ised him and his people personal, national, and universal blessing. Its provisions, however, seemed a far cry from the present
experience of those who were even now invoking God's aid.
The disparity between His promise and their experience would
naturally lead them to ask, "If the Lord could bless Abraham
and fulfill His covenant with him, what must we do to enjoy
similar blessing?"[3] The answer to this question is found in the
example of their forefather. He had obeyed the Lord (see
Genesis 26:5). He had responded in obedience whenever God
revealed His will to him. He had willingly turned his back on
the land of his birth and had journeyed to a strange land he had
never seen before. Throughout his life he had lived in submission to the will of God (Nehemiah 9:8). His example provides the
basis of encouragement for those in Jerusalem. They are acutely conscious of their subservience to the Persians (9:36-38).
God, however, is still the same. He has not changed. Obedience
continues to be the passport to blessing.

The Levites fittingly conclude this section of their prayer by
affirming the righteousness of God. Because of His unchangeable character they know He will deal justly with His
people. If they turn to Him in repentance and faith He will
again show Himself strong on their behalf (see 2 Chronicles
7:14; 15:2).

Lingering Images

In their prayer, the Levites pass on to consider the next
period of Israel's history. They survey the events from the captivity in Egypt to their deliverance under Moses. In doing so,
they dwell on the greatness of God. They remind the people of
His compassion and recount how He broke the might of
Pharaoh, the strongest monarch of the day. They reiterate how
He constituted them a nation at Mount Sinai, graciously guided
them in the trackless desert, and made ample provision for
their needs.

Whereas Abraham set the Israelites an example, this

---

[3] That the blessing of Israel as a nation was conditioned upon obedience is
borne out by such passages as Exodus 19:5; 23:22; Leviticus 26:3-43;
Deuteronomy 7:9,12-15; 11:26-28; 15:4-5; 28:1-14; Psalm 103:17; etc.

rehearsal of their past serves to encourage them with regard to the future. All of God's acts are shown to be signs of His kindness toward them. What is needed, therefore, is for them to return to the just ordinances, true laws, and good statutes which He gave them—the basic foundation without which a nation cannot expect to prosper (Proverbs 14:34).

By reminding the people of God's mighty acts in the past, the Levites create a need in their hearts. They compare their present condition with what God had planned for them, and as they reflect on the way He helped their fathers, they begin to entertain hope for the future.

Playing Games with God

As the Levites continue their prayer they describe the ingratitude, rebellion, and willful disregard for God's Law, which characterized those who settled in the land. God, however, did not cast off His people. He continued to deal with them on the basis of His faithfulness.

As the Jews listen to this reminder of God's long-suffering, they have occasion to think of the way in which their ancestors repudiated the covenant relationship.[4] The history of their people serves to warn them of the consequences of forgetfulness and disobedience. They see how easy it was for their fathers to drift away from the Lord, and are forcefully reminded that those who do not learn the lessons of history are forever condemned to repeat them.

In spite of the faithlessness of their forefathers, the Jews readily see evidence of God's continued faithfulness towards them. He gave them victories and provided them with an inheritance in the land of Canaan. As the Levites recreate in the minds of the Israelites the events of this period they dwell in poetic fashion upon the material blessings their fathers enjoyed. They captured fortified cities and took possession of houses full of good things. They drank from wells they did not

[4] Israel's repudiation of the covenant is seen in verse 18. Not only did they take the first step toward idolatry, but they no longer referred to the deity they worshiped as *Yahweh* (LORD). The word used in this verse is *Elohim*, "God," and its use implies a setting aside of their unique covenant relationship.

dig, and ate from vineyards they did not plant. They "lux-
uriated" themselves in all of God's goodness.

Roadblocks to Renewal

Unfortunately the conquest of the land was never satisfactorily completed. The problem was invariably one of failure to
trust the Lord and obey His command. They also failed to learn
from past mistakes. Sins of omission as well as commission
were repeated continuously. A pattern of willful disobedience
and arrogance prevailed. The Israelites found, however, that
every time history repeated itself, the price went up. Because
they threw God's Law behind their backs, killed the prophets
He sent to them, and committed acts of contempt against Him,
they were given into the hands of oppressors. Enemy nations
plundered their land and became God's instruments to *chasten*
them. When they repented, He graciously delivered them. For
awhile they would walk before Him, but with the death of the
deliverer the cycle of apostasy and oppression would be
repeated. Once again the sons of Israel would have to learn
that disobedience only robbed them of God's best.

After the period of the judges, there came the monarchy.
Saul, David, and Solomon ruled the nation successively. Their
reigns are passed over without mention. When the kingdom
was divided, the northern tribes lasted for a period of 260
years before being taken into captivity by the Assyrians. The
southern tribes continued for a further 135 years, but were
eventually deported by the Babylonians. It was only on account
of God's grace and compassion that they were not utterly consumed. Then, in His gracious good will, He restored them to the
land He had promised to give them. The Temple was rebuilt,
and they themselves had restored the walls.

This review of their national history provides each Jew with
the stimulus of a noble example, the encouragement of what
God has done in the past, the awesome consequences of ingratitude, and the inevitability of chastening if sin goes unconfessed. But most important of all, there is hope for the
future—hope based on the unchangeable character of God.
They see in the present a product of the past and the seed of
the future. Their anticipation now is that the knowledge of past

events will help them avoid the evil and follow the good (1 Corinthians 10:6,11).

The Levites now come to their supplication. They hold out
hope for the future. They base their plea on God's unchangeable character and appeal to Him for help with their
present troubles. They begin by contemplating the nature of
the One with whom they have to do. He is great and mighty,
awesome and powerful (Nehemiah 9:9-11); His fidelity is unquestioned (9:17b-25), and His compassion is boundless
(9:27-31). They invoke His aid.

The prayer of the Levites quite naturally leads the people to
a new commitment of themselves to the One whose favor they
seek. There is in their attitude a desire for a new relationship
with their covenant-keeping God. Only this will satisfy their
spiritual longings and bring to fruition their nationalistic
hopes. They, therefore, decide to make a solemn agreement in
writing and to seal the document with the signatures of the
leaders of the people.[5] In this way they hope to conserve the
quickening of the Spirit which they have experienced, and consolidate the gains of the past few weeks.

Quest for a Useable Future

The importance of history has been attested by Patrick
Henry. He stated, "I have no light to illumine the pathway of
the future save that which falls over my shoulder from the
past." A knowledge of history gives us perspective on our
present-day problems. From history we are able to learn from
the example of those who have preceded us. As Longfellow
pointed out:

> The lives of great men all remind us
> We can make our lives sublime,
> And, departing, leave behind us
> Footsteps on the sands of time.

History encourages us by reminding us of all that God has
done in the lives of others. "We all tread in the footsteps of il-
lustrious men," and from their experiences we learn the

[5] The contents of the covenant will be the subject of our next chapter. Our
concern in treating Nehemiah 9 is to learn the lessons of history.

benefits of godliness and the sorrowful consequences of spiritual waywardness. History also helps us avoid the errors and false practices of men and nations. This is particularly true of Biblical history (see 1 Corinthians 10:6,11). The sons of Israel, for example, could turn their thoughts to the period of the judges and see the recurring cycle of departure from the Lord—discipline—repentance—and deliverance (see Romans 15:4). Seen in this light, the benefits of righteousness, integrity, and morality become obvious.

Secondly, the history of man and his ability to enjoy life— individually as well as nationally—is intimately intertwined with his conformity to the will of God. After observing the testimony of the centuries, Daniel Webster remarked, "If we abide by the principles taught in the Bible, our country will go on prospering and continue to prosper, but if we and our posterity neglect its instructions and authority, no man can tell how sudden a catastrophe may overwhelm us and bury our glory in profound obscurity" (see Proverbs 10:22). There is no adequate substitute for godliness.

Thirdly, from our study of Nehemiah 9 we can take courage from the fact that God is active in history. We may, at times, be tempted to doubt His involvement. The Israelites certainly were not always conscious of His care and loving concern. This, however, did not mean that He was not working behind the scenes (comp. Habakkuk 1:5ff). By observing God's activity in the past, they came to know more of His work in the present. They learned of His *majesty* when they heard Him spoken of as "the great, the mighty, and the terrible God." They came to know more of His *fidelity* through His keeping covenant with them in spite of their faithlessness. And they experienced a revival of hope as they contemplated His *compassion*.

Because God is the same "yesterday and today and forever" (Hebrews 13:8) we too may have confidence as we approach Him. We may have our faith quickened as we think of our past failures and seek His aid for the future. To the extent that we are willing to accept His will for our lives, to that extent we may anticipate His blessing.

A Biblical approach to history will neither make us wide-eyed optimists nor downhearted pessimists. It does give us confidence as we face tomorrow. We see man's triumphs for God and also observe the efforts of those whose lives have produced few tangible results. When this is set against the continuing conflict of good and evil and the downward trend of every civilization since Cain's (Genesis 4:16ff), it leads us realistically to anticipate the future. Such a view corrects our system of values, motivates us to consistent Christian living, and makes the return of Christ an eagerly anticipated event.

TIME FOR REFLECTION

1. In Nehemiah 9:1-4 prominence is given to three things: contrition for and confession of sin; further exhortation from the Word; and worship.

    Why is confession important in the spiritual life? What other passages of Scripture deal with confession of sin?

    What were the effects of hearing Scripture explained in the lives of the Jews? What may we reasonably expect to be our response to reading the Word?

    Why has worship been described as a lost art today? How may it be recovered? What led up to a recovery of worship on the part of those in Jerusalem?

2. When God is seen in His greatness our problems are reduced to size (see Nehemiah 9:6). Of what practical value is the reminder of God's majesty and past activity on behalf of His own?

3. In recounting the history of God's dealings with His people (Nehemiah 9:5-31), the Levites began by leading the people in praise and adoration. Then, in their prayer, they emphasized the blessings of the covenant—blessings which the Israelites had experienced throughout their history. What do you think was the attitude of the people during this prayer? How might their attitude have changed at each different stage of the prayer (9:7-15, 9:16-25, 9:26-31)?

    In what specific ways may their gathering together as the people of God have kindled hope in their hearts? Were these Israelites conscious of failure? Why would the rehearsal of their history have had a quickening effect on them?

4. Nehemiah 9 closes with an earnest plea (9:32-38). The Levites entreat the Lord, in keeping with His personal attributes, to be gracious to them. Confession again appears prominently in the text, for fresh errors of omission and commission have been recalled to their minds. Describe the condition of the people materially and spiritually.

    1 Corinthians 10:5-15 parallels Nehemiah 9:9ff. What specific principles of conduct does the apostle Paul lift from

this narrative and apply to the church? To what extent and in what subtle ways are the same vices permeating the church today?

Something to think about: The Israelites met together with a view to entering into a covenant with the Lord (Nehemiah 9:38). In considering their intentions, think too of one of the greatest Americans of all time, Jonathan Edwards, who likewise made a covenant with the Lord:

I made a solemn dedication of myself to God, and wrote it down; giving up myself and all that I had to God, to be for the future in no respect my own; to act as one that had no right to himself in any respect; and solemnly vowed to take God for my whole portion and felicity, looking on nothing else as any part of my happiness, nor acting as if it were; and His law for the constant rule of my obedience, engaging to fight with all my might against the world, the flesh, and the devil, to the end of my life.

14

TANGIBLE RESULTS

Nehemiah 10

When the Apostle Paul wrote to the Christians in Rome, he exhorted them, "With eyes wide open to the mercies of God . . . give Him your bodies, as a living sacrifice, consecrated to Him and acceptable by Him. . . . Let God remold your minds from within, so that you may prove in practice that the plan of God for you is good, meets all His demands and moves toward the goal of true maturity" (Romans 12:1-2 Phillips).

This idea of being a *living* sacrifice is most interesting. Its appeal is twofold. There is the initial act of consecration as well as the continuous activity, the crisis as well as the process, the gift given to God as well as the life rendered in service.

There is also a major contrast between what the Apostle Paul spoke of and the Old Testament system of sacrifices. The Jews offered up sacrifices that recently had been slaughtered before the altar. Here, the sacrifice placed on the altar is alive. What is involved is offering to God all we are and have and hope to be—for His glory. In Old Testament times, the fire consumed the sacrifice. In Romans 12, Paul has in mind the purifying process which leads to our personal maturity. But there is a snag. When things become too hot we sometimes "get off the altar" and go back on our commitment. Our consecration then becomes incomplete and we do not grow spiritually as we should.

How may this faulty consecration be avoided? The answer is to be found in Nehemiah 10.

In our study of the spirit of renewal which came spontaneously to the Jews, we have seen that it began with a hunger for the Word. Then, with the people once more aware of their standing before God, the religious leaders moved to conserve the results. This move to preserve the spiritual progress which had been made began with a rehearsal of their history. The Levites recounted their past failures and encouraged them to commit themselves afresh to the Lord. All this was done with a view to preparing them for the signing of the covenant. This chapter contains the record of those who signed the covenant (Nehemiah 10:1-27); and the specific content of the covenant (28-39).

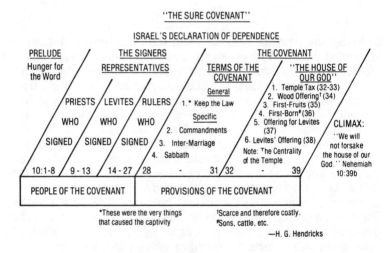

"THE SURE COVENANT"

ISRAEL'S DECLARATION OF DEPENDENCE

PRELUDE	THE SIGNERS	THE COVENANT	
Hunger for the Word	REPRESENTATIVES	TERMS OF THE COVENANT	"THE HOUSE OF OUR GOD"
	PRIESTS / LEVITES / RULERS	*General* 1.* Keep the Law *Specific* 2. Commandments 3. Inter-Marriage 4. Sabbath	1. Temple Tax (32-33) 2. Wood Offering† (34) 3. First-Fruits (35) 4. First-Born# (36) 5. Offering for Levites (37) 6. Levites' Offering (38) Note: The Centrality of the Temple
	WHO / WHO / WHO		CLIMAX: "We will not forsake the house of our God." Nehemiah 10:39b
	SIGNED / SIGNED / SIGNED		
10:1-8 / 9 - 13 / 14 - 27	28 - 31	32 - 39	
PEOPLE OF THE COVENANT	PROVISIONS OF THE COVENANT		

*These were the very things that caused the captivity

†Scarce and therefore costly.
#Sons, cattle, etc.

—H. G. Hendricks

Dynasty of the Committed

The covenant which had been drawn up (probably by Ezra) is now voluntarily accepted by the heads of the nation (Nehemiah 9:38). They have been prepared for this step by two essential prerequisites: (1) A knowledge of what God requires of them. This has come through the reading of the Law. They are keenly aware of His standard and how far short they have fallen. (2) The emotional effect of the review of their history. They see all too clearly how their past failures have brought them to their present condition. However, in spite of God's chastening, they have come to understand that His love still overshadows and protects them. They have also confessed their sins and now they wish to ratify the desire of their hearts. They therefore determine to enter into a covenant[1] with their covenant-keeping God.

Nehemiah, the governor, is the first to set his seal to the document. While he has taken a back seat during this time of spiritual renewal, he now steps forward and sets an example for the others to follow. The next to sign is Zedekiah. He may have been Nehemiah's secretary.[2] They are followed by the priests (Nehemiah 10:2-8), the Levites (10:9-13), and the leaders of the people (10:14-27). Finally, "the rest of the people . . . and all who have separated themselves from the peoples of the lands to the law of God, their wives, their sons, and their daughters, all those who have knowledge and understanding, join with their kinsmen . . . taking on themselves a curse and an oath to walk in God's law . . . and to keep and observe all the commandments of the LORD . . . and His ordinances and His statutes." This represents a significant step forward, particularly if Eliashib, the high priest (signing for the house of Seraiah),[3] and the others who had "sold out" to Sanballat and Tobiah (see Nehemiah 6:10-14) really meant to abide by the conditions of the covenant. Unfortunately, we have no means of gauging the depth of conviction or the reality of the profession of some of these religious leaders (see Nehemiah 13:4-8).

The rest of the people follow the example of the heads of their families. They too have separated themselves *from* the contaminating influence of those around them *to* the law of the Lord. They give their support to those who are attaching their seals to the parchment, signifying thereby their approval and willing acceptance of the terms and conditions of the covenant.

[1] It is significant that the Septuagint (i.e., the translation of the Hebrew Scriptures into Greek) does not use the word *suntheke* (an agreement or covenant between equals) when translating this section, but employs instead the word *diatheke*, a term used to indicate an obligation undertaken by a single party.

[2] Legal documents were normally attested by a scribe and witnesses, with an important official's secretary signing in second place. See J. B. Pritchard's *Ancient Near Eastern Texts* (1959), pp. 219-223.

[3] On the other hand, if Ezra signed for the house of Seraiah, then Eliashib the high priest was among those who refused to sign the covenant (compare Nehemiah 10:2-8 and 12:1-7). *Those following the "and" in 12:6 did not sign the covenant.*

The Pursuit of Ideals

Of primary importance is the covenant itself. There is, first, the decision to submit themselves to the authority of the Scriptures (Nehemiah 10:28-29). They know that they cannot expect God's blessing without being obedient to His Word. They also know that they have to act responsibly before Him. To pray for His blessing and then go their way will not work. Their own history has shown them the result of such foolish logic. Disobedience had brought the inevitable chastening; and the Jews of Nehemiah's time feel that they have suffered enough. They now want God's blessing. Their first commitment, therefore, is to His Word.

This general decision to place themselves under the authority of the Scriptures is not burdensome (see Matthew 11:27-30). By following the teaching of the Lord their lives will be brought into conformity with the truth. The Word of God will become the charter of their liberty, change their system of values, and provide the basis of their government.

From this general statement, the Israelites then pledge themselves to observe certain specifics. They determine to abstain from intermarriage.[4] They have at last begun to realize that by marrying those who do not hold sacred the things which they regard as being important, there has come about a breakdown in the home. Religious differences have resulted in the children being improperly instructed in the way of the Lord (see Nehemiah 13:23-29). This, in turn, has undermined their society. When spiritual realities have been set aside, moral values have deteriorated, and greed, selfishness, and oppression have become the order of the day. This has led to disunity and the deterioration of their national identity.

The condition regulating marriage is followed by one highlighting the importance of worship. The Jews determine to keep the Sabbath, allow the ground to lie fallow each seventh

[4] Their own history has shown them the folly of intermarriage. See Exodus 23:32-33; 34:12-16; Deuteronomy 7:3; Joshua 23:12-13; Judges 3:6-8; 1 Kings 11:4; Ezra 9:2.

year, and cancel all debts.[5] They also pledge themselves to maintain the Temple and those who minister in it (Nehemiah 10:32-39).[6] God's House is once again the center of their lives. Not only will they insure that the required sacrifices are offered, but they will also make certain that there is an adequate supply of wood. Furthermore the extent of the Lord's claim on their lives will touch all they have—their children, cattle, produce, and even the new wine and oil.

In the handling of the revenue of the Temple, a priest is to join with a Levite when the tithes are received. In this way, both groups will be represented and the priests will be assured of their share.

Finally, on a note of great solemnity, all the people affirm that "they will not neglect the house of their God" (Nehemiah 10:39b). Without a strong religious center, the nation will not long survive. Their enemies are too strong for them. They need the kind of help which comes from their covenant-keeping God if the society they are establishing is to endure.

And so the covenant is signed.

The Unchanging Foundation

With this resume of the conditions of the covenant, the second division of the book (containing the spiritual instruction of the people [Nehemiah 8—10]) comes to a close. It is interesting to notice that the movement that began with the people requesting to be taught the Word of the Lord, ends with the leaders laying down a sound theological foundation for the future.

But was this really necessary? Why impose these obligations on them? Wouldn't they inhibit the laity and limit the working of the Spirit?

[5] The Sabbath, Exodus 20:8-11; Deuteronomy 5:12-15; sabbatical years, Exodus 23:10-11; compare Leviticus 25:2-7; Deuteronomy 15:1-18; the canceling of all debts, Exodus 21:7; 22:25-27; Leviticus 25:39-40; Deuteronomy 15:10-13. See R. DeVaux, *Ancient Israel* (1961), pp.475-482.

[6] The Old Testament Scriptures are permeated with passages relating to the different items mentioned in these verses. See Exodus 25:30; 39:38-42; Leviticus 4:1-5; 6:12ff; 23; 24:5-9; 25:2-7; Numbers 15:22-29; 28:3—29:9; etc. See also R. DeVaux, *Ancient Israel* (1961), pp.322-330,387-405.

No work for the Lord can advance and prosper without enthusiasm. Traditionally this has come from the laity. There is, however, a need to temper zeal with knowledge. Without a proper doctrinal basis we might easily become guilty of an excess of enthusiasm, or alternatively enforce a rigid set of rules. The Church in Corinth was guilty of the former and abused the gifts of the Spirit that had been given to them. The Judaizers within the early Church were guilty of the latter and, had the Apostle Paul not corrected their false teaching, the Church might have been plunged into legalism. Unfortunately, an excess of enthusiasm frequently results in antinomianism, while the opposite extreme degenerates into religious bigotry and man-made dogmas. The movement on the part of laymen of Israel needed the guidance of a well-trained theologian such as Ezra. The leaders in Jerusalem wisely combined enthusiasm with sound doctrine. Zeal was merged with knowledge and knowledge was given practical emphasis by being allied with zeal.

It should also be pointed out that the people readily accepted the conditions of the covenant (Nehemiah 10:29). As we look back on their position from our unique situation in Christ, we are astounded at the Jewish love of the Law, and we rejoice in our freedom from its irksome restraints. The history of the Church, however, is filled with records of those who have entered into covenants with the Lord. A careful reading of *The Religious Affections* by Jonathan Edwards, or the *Diary of David Brainard* will reveal the kind of obligations devout people willingly took upon themselves. In recent days Dr. George Sweeting, president of Moody Bible Institute, has seen fit to tell of his experience in *Love is the Greatest.* In this book he recounts how one morning he became acutely aware of his own personal failure. As he knelt before the Lord he came to see himself as never before. He poured out his heart in confession and entreaty. In that time of brokenness he vowed not to allow anything to hinder the development of grace in his heart and life. He made the love of God his aim and it became both the foundation and superstructure of his life. Now, in *Love is the Greatest,* he shares with us the way in which we too may enjoy this experience.

Israel's covenant with the Lord contains important prin-

ciples for all of us. At its very base was, to borrow William
Gladstone's phrase, "the impregnable rock of Holy Scripture."
The Jews established their beliefs as well as their practices
upon the infallible revelation of God. This kept them from succumbing to the fallible theories of man—no matter how plausible they might sound.

This commitment to the Scriptures as the only reliable
authority in all matters of faith and practice is precisely what
we need today. The authority of the Bible has been attacked by
"friends" within the church and foes without. In spite of all the
criticisms, it stands as God's Word written. To all who will accept it, it becomes a sure and certain guide to all the many and
varied contingencies of life. By following its teaching, we enjoy
far more than we could ever extract from all the world's
wisdom (see Psalm 119:97ff; John 8:32,36). It brings all of life into perspective. Obedience to its teaching becomes the basis of
God's blessing, whether of the individual or of the nation. As
Dr. Merrill F. Unger correctly observed, "A contagious enthusiasm among Christians for the Word of God and a return to
faith and obedience to its precepts will do more to point the
way out of the present world distress and despair than all the
plans and strivings of men." We can no more afford to neglect
the Word of God than could the Israelites of Nehemiah's time.
We should read it eagerly, ever mindful of its Author, message,
and relevance to our daily lives. And we should diligently obey
it and regard each imperative as God's supreme command.

As we look back over the chapter, a second principle
emerges. It centers in the purity God expects of His people. To
be sure, there is the cleansing action of the Word on our lives
(Psalm 119:9). But there is also its impact on society. In the
response of the Jews to the Word, they separated themselves
from the degrading influence of the idolators who lived among
them. The religious practices of these people were particularly
licentious and exceedingly detrimental to the moral life of the
nation. As we apply this principle of separation to our own
situation, we need to remember that "evil communications corrupt good manners." Whereas God expects us to live *in* the
world, He does not want us to be *of* it (John 17:4-16; 1 Peter
1:15-16).

Separation, however, should never be solely negative. The

Jews of Nehemiah's time separated themselves from those about them to the Word of the Lord. This added a positive dimension to what they were doing. Those who had publicly indicated their desire to abide by the conditions of the covenant became the company of the committed. They could enjoy fellowship with each other on a richer, more rewarding level. They could edify each other and build one another up in the faith. The same principle applies to us today. In fact, this is what fellowship is all about. But this fellowship is not to be with the unfruitful works of darkness (Ephesians 5:11). Rather it is with the Father and the Son, and with those whose lives are ordered by the truth (1 John 1:3,5-7).

Thirdly, the Israelites also felt the need to maintain the Temple and its services. Those responsible for drafting the covenant were aware of the peril of moral and spiritual ignorance. They saw the strong link between the religious training of the people and their social conduct, and they knew that without adequate leadership the people would speedily lapse into spiritual ignorance and moral torpor. The Temple and its services were to become the center of their lives and they, in turn, pledged themselves to maintain its worship.

It would be easy for us, in our milieu, to substitute the local church for the Temple. To do so, however, would lead to confusion and theological error. The New Testament tells us that our bodies (not the local church!) are the temple of the Holy Spirit (1 Corinthians 3:16-17; 16:19; 2 Corinthians 6:16). Believers, individually, are being built up together into a temple of the Lord (Ephesians 2:21-22; 4:15-16; 1 Peter 2:5). God still desires to be the center of our lives. Now, however, He indwells us. Instead of worshiping externally in a material sanctuary, worship is now internal. It is the heart's response to God (see John 4:21,23-24). The local church may still be a powerful force for good in the community, but it should not be regarded as the New Testament counterpart of the Old Testament sanctuary.

Even with all of these blessings and provisions, many of us still become far more preoccupied with the *external things* of life than with the *internal realities*. The full impact of the spiritual dimension of believers becoming the temple of God seems intangible and hard for us to grasp. However, the more we dwell on the indwelling ministry of the Spirit of God, the better will be our understanding of the privilege all born-again believers enjoy.

As we look back over this section, it is gratifying to see the course taken as the people responded to the movement of God's Spirit in their midst. As we too yield to His will, we will find that He produces in us the same kind of obedience to the Word, high moral standards, genuine concern for the things of the Lord, and desire to look after the material welfare of those who minister to us in Christ's stead!

TIME FOR REFLECTION

1. Note from Nehemiah 10:1 that leaders lead best by example. What excuses might Nehemiah have offered for noninvolvement in the events of chapters 8–10? What indication is there that Nehemiah was very much involved in what was taking place, but without getting in the way of the priests and the Levites (see also 8:9ff.)?

   Notice that twenty-four priests, seventeen Levites, and forty-four heads of families likewise set an example for the people. What is the result of their actions on the masses (Nehemiah 10:28)?

2. In ordering their priorities, those signing the covenant committed themselves to "walk in God's law." How was their commitment to be worked out in practice? What areas of their lives would be involved? Why was intermarriage expressly forbidden? How does this commandment underscore the importance of maintaining a godly home?

3. Why was it easy for the Jews to minimize the importance of observing the sabbath (Nehemiah 10:31)? What did observance of the sabbatical year imply for the Jews (Exodus 20:8-10; Leviticus 25:1-7; Deuteronomy 5:15; 15:1-4; Psalm 24:1)?

4. Discuss the various ways in which support of the Temple was insured (Nehemiah 10:34-39). What was the most difficult commodity to supply? Why? In what ways may the items to be given to the Temple parallel our stewardship today? What principles apply to our support of the Lord's work?

   Why is it easy to become preoccupied with externals so that we neglect the dwelling place of God today (1 Corinthians 6:10-20)? How may the temple within us be maintained? Do the items of the covenant (Nehemiah 10:28-33) have any application to us today in terms of maintaining our spiritual vitality? In what ways is it easy to neglect our spiritual natures?

Something to think about: Maintaining a Christian home is vitally important. The Bible does not say very much about homes per se; it does say a great deal about the things which make them. It speaks about life and love, joy and peace, human relationships and mutual submission. These are the things that make a house a home . . . and a fit place in which to rear our children (1 Timothy 4:8b).

15

THE NEW BEGINNING

Nehemiah 11

Do you remember the time you and your friends constructed your first tree house or converted an old shed into your private den? You were about ten or eleven years old and had all the confidence in the world. And do you remember the arguments you had—sometimes boisterous and always vocal—as you elected your first leader, established the rules of membership ("No Girls"), and formalized the rites of initiation?

In those days, you and your friends tacitly showed the need for some formal organization. The election of a leader was an admission of the need you all felt for *authority,* and his "election" invested him with certain *power.* At that age you would have spurned all thought of *control,* and yet the rules you agreed upon implied certain limitations; and your concurrence intimated your *consent.* Then came the delegation of *responsibility*—who would do the different chores. All of this was followed by those idyllic afternoons when you and your friends reveled in the delights of your temporary autonomy (you had to be home by five).

In those days—now largely forgotten with the advance of the years—you laid the foundation of your own administration or "government." In fact, the needs you felt and set about meeting are the same kind that face mankind everywhere. Our social instincts lead us to band together. Wherever we attempt to work together through an organization, a form of government arises. In establishing its administration there must, of necessity, be the *consent* of all concerned, the acceptance of *controls,* the extent and limitations of *power,* and the reciprocal conferring of *authority* with the acceptance of *responsibility.*

But theories of governance—whether of a church, a corporation, a club, or a group—conflict. Ideologies are found to be contradictory. What was originally designed "for the public good" degenerates into lust for and abuse of power.

With all the confusion that surrounds us, it is important for us to know what the Bible teaches on the subject. In this respect, Nehemiah 11 deals with the establishment of a new form of society. All of this follows quite naturally the building of the walls (Nehemiah 1—6), and the spiritual instruction of the people (8—10).

Innovation and Organization

The work that Nehemiah began when he took a census of the people (Nehemiah 7) can now continue. The sparse population of the capital constitutes a major problem. The city is vulnerable and can easily be overrun by its enemies. The leaders of the people, of course, live in Jerusalem. They control the commerce and industry. The majority of the people, however, live in the outlying towns and villages.

In the event of an attack, Jerusalem would be a particularly dangerous place in which to live. A farmer living in reasonable proximity to the city, might have his crops plundered and his herds driven off, but he and his family could, in all probability, escape with their lives by hiding from the invaders. In a similar way, people living in the outlying towns would be able to hide in the hills as soon as a band of marauders came into their vicinity. Not so with those living in Jerusalem. The capital would become the focal point of an attack. Furthermore, those residing in the city found it to be a post of labor as well as danger. The fortifications required constant guarding and this imposed additional responsibilities on the citizenry.

In planning for the repopulation of Jerusalem, Nehemiah could have arbitrarily demanded that certain families sell their homes or farms and move to the city. This, however, was not his way. The decision on how to effect the urban renewal of the city comes from the people. Some of the Jews, who are now more aware of their spiritual heritage than ever before, volunteer to move into the city. This is a mark of patriotism as well as self-denial.

The second step in repopulating the capital takes the form of public action. "The people cast lots to bring one out of every ten to live in Jerusalem, the holy city, while nine-tenths [remain] in the other cities." In view of the census already taken (Nehemiah 7), it appears as if Nehemiah explained the need to the leaders of the different towns and villages. They, in turn, must have called "town meetings" to discuss the best means of meeting the need. The people respond positively to this kind of approach and *they* decide upon a method of repopulating Jerusalem.

The inner dynamics backing up this decision are of great importance. They originate in the pride each Jew feels now that Jerusalem is again defendable. The wall around the city gives them a sense of national identity. With this rekindling of a nationalistic spirit there is a new awareness of their relationship to God. They are His covenant people and secure in their standing before Him. They speak of Jerusalem as "the holy city" and, by casting lots, determine who shall move to the capital. Their casting of lots shows their submission to the will of God (Proverbs 16:33). [1]

In the absence of a king in Judah, and God's rule over His people through a local (theocratic) representative, a form of democracy prevails. It is a democracy established upon a strong religious foundation. Normatively there is justice, equity, and equality. Structurally there is a distribution of power with the people sharing in the affairs of their community. Behaviorally there is an absence of conflict. All of this finds its origin in the relationship of the people to the Lord and their desire to do His will.

Pattern and Process

From this general statement of the principle by which the urban renewal of Jerusalem is accomplished, Nehemiah lists the families who make up the new residency. What may at first

---

[1] In Israel, the casting of lots was a means the people used to determine the will of God (Numbers 26:55-56; Joshua 7:16,18: 1 Samuel 10:19-21; 1 Chronicles 24:5; 25:8). Other ancient civilizations also used this kind of strategy (e.g., in Greece, to determine between candidates for public office) but none with the guarantee of divine approval.

sight be regarded as another dry rehearsal of names, takes on new significance when we consider the political structure and administration of the city. Two different groups are mentioned in Nehemiah 11:4-9. They represent two separate tribes. Judah is a large tribe and Benjamin is a small tribe. In fact, from the time of the divided kingdom, the tribe of Benjamin had been included in the southern kingdom under the title "Judah." It was only natural that their individual identity would gradually be eroded. Furthermore, the sons of Perez have a long and enviable history (Numbers 26:21; 1 Chronicles 27:3). They are looked up to and respected, and are accustomed to having their own way. The people of Benjamin, on the other hand, are renowned for their savage bravery and skill in war (Genesis 49:27; Judges 3:15; 20:16; 1 Chronicles 8:40). Now that they begin to feel the first resurgence of tribal pride, they are not likely to take kindly to others dictating the terms to them. How then may these factions work together when each is seeking to establish itself in a new environment? By what means will they be able to adjust to each other?

The whole matter of the administration of the city is further complicated by the fact that only a few weeks before, Nehemiah had appointed new leaders over Jerusalem (Nehemiah 7:2). Hanani and Hananiah have hardly had time to settle into their new roles when these newcomers begin to arrive. These new residents can only have added to the strain already felt by these men.

Nehemiah's handling of the problem of the new residents is explained in Nehemiah 11:9. Whether the leaders mentioned in the text were appointed by Nehemiah or elected by the people is not stated. We have already seen how Nehemiah preferred a democratic form of election. Regardless of the method by which they were chosen, these men are obviously acceptable to the people. Inasmuch as Hanani has been placed over the city, Joel is probably responsible to him; and Judah may have been answerable directly to Hananiah, the commander of the fortress.[2] In any event, two important principles are seen in

[2] Nehemiah 11:9 is not only difficult to translate, it is difficult to interpret as well. If Joel represented only the Benjaminites, who represented the people of Judah? If Judah, the son of Hassinuah, was second in command of the city, who was first in command? The phrase "second in command" could yield the mean-

Nehemiah's handling of the move. First, in seeking the happiness of the people, Nehemiah obviously bases his administration on equity and equality; and secondly, there is adequate representation of the people through their representatives.

Normatively, these groups (and the individuals within them) make up a new social system. Their leaders have authority given to them and are held accountable for the way in which they carry out their duties. They assess the mood of the people and represent them to their immediate superiors.

Structurally, there is adequate subordination (i.e., a concise chain of command) and a clear distinction of job function. Each man has jurisdiction over his own group and each is responsible to his immediate superior for the well-being of those under his control. There is also representation on a broad enough base so that each group feels that its voice is being heard.

From a behavioral point of view, there is an absence of the usual kind of altercations that accompany a large-scale disruption of families. There can be little doubt that the reality of their religious experience led the people to subordinate their own personal desires and seek the good of others. They willingly submerge their personal differences and work together to achieve harmony and proper *esprit de corps*.

Ritual, Ruts, and Rebellion

Further examination of this chapter shows that other groups choose to come and live in the city of Jerusalem. Among these are the priests who serve in the Temple (Nehemiah 11:10-14), Levites who are in charge of the outside work of the House of God (11:15-18,22-24), and gatekeepers and temple servants (11:19-21). These groups already have their regularly constituted leaders, and Nehemiah works through them without appointing representatives of his own choosing.

ing "was over the second quarter" of the city (see 2 Kings 22:14). It seems preferable, therefore, to interpret this section in the light of 7:1-4. When this is done, adequate *division of responsibility*, as well as proper *subordination of authority*, is the result.

It should be observed, however, that the inclusion of these specialized groups in the new residency of Jerusalem could easily have posed a threat to the administrators of the capital. The priests, by virtue of their position as religious leaders, already wield great power over the people. They are not particularly well disposed, or even loyal, to the new governor. In the absence of some overriding concern, they might be inclined to give him, and those whom he has appointed to positions of responsibility, little more than lip service. We know that there are some in the high priest's family who are more interested in the economy and their own material prosperity than they are in spiritual matters. These could easily arrive at policy decisions contrary to the principles already established by the governor (e.g., Nehemiah 7:3-4; 13:19-22). Lobbying to create public agitation could result in dissatisfaction with Nehemiah's administration.

It is interesting to notice that, in spite of Israel's unique relationship to God, Nehemiah does not build his administration upon the priesthood. Political and religious entities are kept separate. Israel's spiritual heritage forms the basis of their governmental system and regulates their ethical standards, but the priests do not rule the people! Nehemiah differentiates between religious duties and secular concerns, and he is wise enough to use this natural division in the apportionment of responsibility and in dividing the administrative responsibility of the city. To do otherwise would only hinder the work of consolidation.

And what of the Levites, gatekeepers, and other temple servants? They are also descendants of Aaron but, in contrast to their priestly brethren, are held responsible for the *outside* work of the House of the Lord. Do they feel inferior? Will this lead to a smoldering resentment which will find other ways of expressing itself?

All of this could make it easy for Nehemiah and his subordinates to feel threatened by the new arrivals.

In the place of a secular democracy, Nehemiah shows how a form of government—established upon sound Biblical principles—can and should operate. The difficulties that easily might have arisen are avoided because of the people's recent spiritual awakening.

Source of Strength

Finally, in establishing his new form of administration, Nehemiah displays the inward strength which must, of necessity, characterize all successful administrators. His confidence is in the Lord. Those who might have constituted a threat to his security do not do so because of his implicit faith and trust in the One who called him to undertake this task.

Insecurity arises when people, for one reason or another, fail to feel a part of a group, suffer from a poor estimate of their work, or lack confidence in themselves. Christians are particularly prone to suffer from one or more of these traits. Fortunately for us, God has made adequate provision for our needs. The love of the Father for us is such that He sent the Lord Jesus into the world so that, through His death, we may become members of His family (John 1:12-14). As previously mentioned, this gives us a sense of *belonging*. When we accept the Lord Jesus as our Saviour, God the Father adopts us as His children and makes us, not only His heirs, but joint heirs with Christ as well. This gives us a sense of *worth*. At conversion the Holy Spirit Himself comes and indwells us; and with His power at work in our lives we are made equal to every task. This makes us *competent*. And the sense of belonging, the realization of our worth, and the knowledge of the Holy Spirit's indwelling provides us with the security we need in our work, and in our relationships with others.

While Nehemiah did not enjoy the full understanding of all that God has provided for us, he was inwardly secure and was confident that the Lord would see him safely through each crisis.

Innovative Administration

The chapter closes with a recounting of those towns and villages surrounding Jerusalem that belong to the tribes of Judah and Benjamin. To the casual reader, this may seem like another list of names that easily can be passed over. Their very enumeration, however, coming as it does at the end of a chapter devoted to the political government of the people, elicits another important principle. Nehemiah's administration cut across conventional lines. He followed a decentralized form of administration. Each city and village was responsible for its own government. His practice was in marked contrast to the established policy of his day which emphasized a strong central government. In a centralized authority (as in an absolute monarchy [such as Artaxerxes'], a dictatorship, an oligarchy, or a junta) where the power is concentrated in a select few and where the usual checks and balances are minimal, there is a ready climate for intrigue and strife. In Nehemiah's administration, power was generated by the public through the aggregation of their political needs. These needs were made known to appointed officials through leaders elected by each group. Whereas this might seem like an early form of the Roman *Vox populi, vox Dei* ("The voice of the people is the voice of God"), Nehemiah's administration differed from Rome's in that in Judah there was a strong commitment to Biblical principles. By building upon a well-established, ethical (religious) foundation, Nehemiah formed a democratic state with a decentralized authority. He could not have succeeded in this had God not interrupted his earlier attempt at consolidation with a spiritual awakening among the people.

A strong religious commitment is essential if a democratic form of administration is to succeed. Without adequate spiritual values it is hard, if not impossible, to retain the idea of obligation and responsibility. Individualism cannot long be held in check by the concept of a calling embodying good works and self-restraint. When this control is weakened, legislation takes the place of spiritual convictions and becomes the foundation of the community. And with the increase in legislation there is a corresponding increase in bureaucracy with a minimizing of efficiency and a diminution of personal worth.

The principles that Nehemiah employed to govern the people of God apply to corporations, church groups, professional bodies, clubs, trade unions, cooperative movements, educational organizations, and any other kind of corporate venture. They all need sound democratic regulation, and the basic principles Nehemiah used are worth following.

It is fine for us (with our 20 x 20 "hindsight") to conclude that so far Nehemiah has been extremely successful. Under his capable leadership, there has come about a revival of national prestige. A once downtrodden people are now able to hold their heads high and look their neighbors in the eye. To this has been added a new spiritual awareness. The people are confident of their standing before God. They are happy in the assurance that they belong to Him. With these remarkable gains, it would be quite natural for a leader to congratulate himself on his successes and settle down to a period of relatively tranquil administration. One thing, however, remains: the integration of those in Jerusalem into a unified group. Lest we entertain the idea that this is unimportant, perhaps we should remember that this is where so many of our churches and organizations fail! People come in looking for warmth and fellowship, a place to belong and a sense of security. Because we fail to make them feel an integral part of what is going on they soon leave us, often feeling disillusioned, disappointed, and worse off for their experience. Exactly how the newcomers are made to feel a part of the entire community will be dealt with next.

TIME FOR REFLECTION

1. William Fulbright, while he was still senator of Arkansas, went on record as saying, "Our theory of democracy has failed. It is time we looked to other nations for a more workable theory of government." More recently the well-respected sociologist from Harvard University, Dr. David Riesman, commented, "The question is not whether [our] leadership is obsolete but whether democracy is governable." What is your opinion?

   If you, as a Christian leader, were to construct your own theory of government (or administration), where would you begin? What would you build into your theory? How would you safeguard people's rights?

   How did God lead Nehemiah to establish the administration of Jerusalem and Judah? What kind of leaders were chosen to look after the interests of the people? How might these leaders have contributed to either the problem or the solution?

2. List the ways the influx of people or already-established power structures could have caused problems for the governor and/or those whom he appointed to positions of leadership. How did Nehemiah avoid these difficulties?

   Can you apply Nehemiah's principles of democratic representation to your situation at work? How far should these principles be taken? What checks and balances are needed so that employees have both freedom of expression and personal responsibility?

3. Of what practical value in our offices or places of business are the following: subordination; a clear distinction of job function; and the delegation of authority commensurate with one's responsibility? How did Nehemiah achieve these?

4. Politicians expect and plan for opposition. They anticipate (sometimes hostile) reactions to their proposals and therefore build the tactics of pressure and compromise into their manipulative schemes. Why was it unnecessary for Nehemiah

to use these tactics?

Had the spirit of renewal done anything to change the people and their goals? Do we need a similar renewal in this country for democracy to work? How could a spiritual renewal be achieved?

Something to think about: Dr. Robert Culver, in *Toward a Biblical View of Civil Government*, concluded:

If Christian influence on government is to be successful in promotion of durable improvements, then the church must be effective in performing its own distinct God-given commission, making disciples—hopefully very many of them (Matthew 28:19-20)—who shall in turn honor Jesus Christ as Lord in every sphere of their lives and who will understand the meaning for the nations of all that Christ in the Scriptures has taught them to observe (Matthew 28:20).

16

TURN OF THE TIDE

Nehemiah 12:1—13:3

Each one of us tries to find meaning in life. We need and seek for cohesion. Our search stems from a desire to secure an ideal. This frequently leads us through different crises, and these crises help us progress toward maturity.

In Christian circles we tend to place a great deal of emphasis on the crises of our experience and pay very little attention to the process that follows. Take, for example, the case of the young person who goes off to a Christian camp. He hears of the claims of Christ on his life and commits himself entirely to the Lord. His search for reality, his efforts to find a basis of authority, and his inner sense of values, are all changed. This is the crisis. It gives him direction and purpose in life. But now there comes the process. As a result of his experience, he has the identity he sought. Life now has meaning. He begins to grow towards spiritual maturity.

What brought about the change in his life? Was it the camp? No. The camp was incidental. It was the message he heard and his response to it.

In Nehemiah 12, the sons of Israel join together to dedicate the wall of Jerusalem. This dedication marks not only the culmination of their labors, but like the summer camp, it is a high point in their experience. It also lays the foundation for future progress.

Faces of Authority

Our chapter opens with another list of names. It shows Nehemiah's concern to maintain the authentic traditions of his people.[1] He goes back to Zerubbabel (ninety years earlier) and surveys the history of the priestly and Levitical families to his own time. In rehearsing these names, specific mention is made of the high priests from Jeshua to Jaddua.

Nehemiah's list has given rise to the charges of inaccuracy in the Biblical record. According to the Jewish historian Josephus, Jaddua lived in the time of Alexander the Great and died about 330 B.C. It was therefore impossible for Nehemiah to be acquainted with Jaddua unless his administration came much *later* than what the Bible indicates. This has led some Bible critics to claim that Nehemiah's governorship of Judah could not have occurred before 404-359 B.C. They do this to make Nehemiah's administration continue to the time when Jaddua began his ministry as high priest. This view, however, is not supported by the evidence at hand. First, it is contrary to the historical data found in Nehemiah's "Memoirs" (Nehemiah 1:1; 2:1; 5:14; 13:6). The reign of Artaxerxes I has been fixed with great accuracy, and Nehemiah's governorship may confidently be dated from 444 B.C. Secondly, evidence from the *Elephantine Papyri* (407 B.C.) dates the high priesthood of Eliashib's grandson at the time when Sanballat's descendants ruled over Samaria. Nehemiah could not have served in Jerusalem to the time of Jaddua (359 B.C.) because he was a contemporary of Eliashib and Sanballat. His administration ran concurrently with Eliashib's and well before 407 B.C.

Other critics date Nehemiah's administration during the reign of Artaxerxes, but claim that the book that bears his name was written long after his death. They try to solve the chronological problems by claiming that the writer or compiler of Nehemiah's "Memoirs" knew of Jaddua and therefore these recollections could not have come from the pen of Nehemiah.

In answering these assertions it should be pointed out that those who try to find errors in the passage rely more heavily on Josephus' testimony than they do on the Scriptures. Josephus' history, moreover, is far from trustworthy. His information is garbled and his chronology confused. In the same chapter in which he mentions Jaddua and Alex-

---

[1] The inclusion of the word "*and*" in verse 6 is significant. When this passage is compared with Nehemiah 10, it appears as if the names which follow "and" represent those of the high priest families who did *not* sign the covenant.

ander the Great as being contemporaries, he shows his untrustworthiness by linking Jaddua with Sanballat and Manasseh (see Nehemiah 13:28). In actual fact, their administrations were separated by more than fifty years! On the other hand, we may account for the inclusion of Jaddua in Nehemiah's record because more than one high priest may have borne this name. It was common practice for Jewish people to give their sons the name of a father or grandfather. In the period of time from Eliashib to Alexander the Great, several priests of the high priest's family may have borne the name Jaddua, so why must we opt for the most unlikely one?

Those critics who claim that Nehemiah could not have compiled his "Memoirs" conveniently ignore the sections in which the governor speaks in the first person. They try to find support for their theory by referring to 12:22. In this verse, mention is made of "Darius, the Persian." Those who claim a late date for the book conclude that this must have been Darius III (335-331 B.C.). But why pass over Darius II (423-404 B.C.)? A chronicler wishing to distinguish between the first Darius ("the Mede" of Daniel 6) would be far more likely to refer to Darius II as "the Persian."[2]

On the basis of the data at hand, there is no evidence that would lead us to date the administration of Nehemiah later than what the Bible attests, or to attribute to the work of an editor the final composition of his book.

Teachers of the Great

As we examine the text, we are reminded afresh of the importance of those who have labored for the Lord before us. We are encouraged by their noble example. Their lives should motivate us to follow the good and pursue the right (Philippians 4:8).

As is invariably the case, the priests are mentioned first (Nehemiah 12:1-21). Their record is followed by a tabulation of the Levites and their families (12:22-26). This register reminds us of the importance and power of godliness in the

[2] For a more detailed discussion of the problem, see Gleason L. Archer's *Survey of the Old Testament Introduction* (1974), pp.410-416.

life of the nation. Many of the common people may have been ignorant of their spiritual heritage.

In this respect, the New Testament has some interesting things to say about our need to become personally acquainted with those who have the responsibility of our spiritual leadership (see Hebrews 13:7,17). We are admonished to remember the former teachers of the Church and not only imitate their faith, but emulate their willingness to suffer for the cause of Christ. After all, it is largely through their labors that we have come under the sound of the gospel. Fortunately, this is not difficult for us to do. A study of church history and the reading of the biographies of the great men of the past will help us appreciate our spiritual heritage.[3] No one can read the writings of the late J. H. Merle D'Aubigne and be the same afterwards.[4] I have found that learning more of men such as Francis Asbury, John Brown of Haddington, Robert Bruce, John Calvin, William Culbertson, V. Raymond Edman, Jonathan Edwards, Charles Hodge, C. H. Spurgeon, John and Charles Wesley, and George Whitefield, and the reading of missionary biographies has done a great deal to stimulate my own faith.

In addition, the Scripture calls upon us to be obedient to those responsible for the well-being of the Church. Those who have the oversight of the Church have undertaken a serious task. They are *shepherds* who must one day give an account of their service to the *Great Shepherd*. We can make their task easier by cooperating with them in the work of the Lord.

Unmolding the Status Quo

Chapter 12 also teaches us that there are different kinds of ministries. Every priest in Israel could not be the high priest.

[3] One of the finest single volume church histories available today is Earle E. Cairns' *Christianity Through the Centuries* (1954).

[4] D'Aubigne was an evangelical French theologian and achieved justifiable fame for his *History of the Reformation in Europe* and *History of the Reformation in England.* Material taken from his *History of the Reformation in the Sixteenth Century* has been incorporated into the popular *Life and Times of Martin Luther.*

Because of their number, David had divided the priesthood into courses. They did not minister all the time. To some were assigned menial tasks, while others enjoyed more prestigious duties. In the diversification of the ministry, some worked inside the Temple while others served outside of it. Those who worked outside were also descendants of the tribe of Levi (Exodus 6:25). They included the gatekeepers, the singers, and the temple servants. *Each one, however, was important. Each one contributed to the work of the whole. And the over-all result was that God was glorified.*

In Ephesians 4, the Apostle Paul tells us that Christ has given gifts to His Church. Some served the early believers as apostles and prophets, others as evangelists and pastor-teachers. All contributed to the edification of the Body of Christ.

Elsewhere in his writing Paul mentions that each believer has been given some spiritual gift (1 Corinthians 12:4-11). Not everyone has the same gift (1 Corinthians 12:12-30). The Holy Spirit bestows His gifts in accordance with His sovereign will. He then works in us and enables us to use our gifts for the edification of others and to advance the cause of Christ. In developing his theme, Paul likens the diversity of gifts to the parts of the body. Not everyone has the same function. Each member needs the other members if he is to operate effectively. In the same way that some Levites were gatekeepers and singers, and others collected the tithes, so today we have diverse ways in which people can use their particular gifts. Some members in our churches are ushers, visit the sick, care for the finances, or promote the tape ministry. Others teach in the Sunday school, serve on committees, maintain the facilities, or sing in the choir. All are important. All are to work together for the greater glory of God.

The Importance of Remembrance

Having stressed the importance of the Jews knowing those who have the rule over them, and having included in his record the different groups of people who served the Temple, Nehemiah now comes to the dedication of the wall. For this solemn, yet joyful occasion, the priests and the Levites purify themselves. In doing so, they *set themselves apart* to God. Their purification probably involves fasting and abstaining from sexual intercourse.[5]

There is nothing sinful about eating or sex.[6] By abstaining from these pleasures, the priests and Levites are saying in effect, "Lord, You are first in my life." The culminating point of their purification is reached at the end of the week when they offer a sin offering.

The purification process extends to the people, the gates of the city, and the wall itself. The people probably wash their clothes (Exodus 19:10,14) and bathe themselves (Numbers 8:5-8; 19:12,19; Ezekiel 36:25). The gates and the wall of the city are ritually cleansed with hyssop (2 Chronicles 29:5ff; Leviticus 14:48-53). All of this is done to remind the Israelites that they and all that they have, belong to the Lord in a special way.

When everything is ready, Nehemiah divides the people and their leaders, the priests and the Levites, into two groups. These groups form two large choirs. With Ezra at the head of one group and Nehemiah leading the other, they walk through the streets, mount the walls, circle the city, and meet together over against the Temple. There, surrounding the temple area, these choirs engage in a responsive anthem. Their antiphonal chorus is heard a great way off. Also on that day, they offer great sacrifices,[7] and rejoice because God has given them great joy. Even the women and children rejoice so that the sound of their rejoicing is heard from afar (Nehemiah 12:43; see also Isaiah 60:18; Zechariah 4:10).

The dedication of the wall is the climax to the months of hardship the people have endured. However, it is more than an

[5] See Genesis 25:2ff; Numbers 8:21ff; 1 Chronicles 15:14; 2 Chronicles 29:15; 35:6; Ezra 6:20; Nehemiah 13:22; Malachi 3:3.

[6] In 1 Corinthians 7:1-5, the Apostle Paul provides similar guidelines for this kind of conduct. He emphasizes the fact that believers are to *stop depriving one another of their conjugal rights, except by agreement for a limited period of time in order that they may devote themselves to prayer. Then they are to come together again lest Satan tempt them because of the lack of self-control.* Sex is God's idea. It is a vital part of every marriage relationship. Abstaining from it should therefore be by mutual consent and solely for the purpose of devoting ourselves unreservedly to prayer. Abstinence should also be for a limited time only.

[7] Probably thank offerings.

initiation. Like a camp at which one may give his life unreservedly to Christ, the dedication of the wall marks a new beginning. As a result, the people receive new identity. They have walked around the very walls they helped to build. This experience welds them together and gives them a sense of accomplishment. Furthermore, the whole ceremony serves to establish their confidence in the Lord. He has helped them, even though at times they had thought of quitting.

During the years I was in college, I had the opportunity of seeing firsthand what happens in this kind of situation. The school I attended was run by the Methodist church and, like many other Christian colleges, was long on faith but short on funds. As students we wanted very badly to have a swimming pool. For many months, after lectures were over, we spent our afternoons digging at the site marked on the architect's plans for a "future" pool. There was no heavy earth-moving equipment available; only picks and shovels. Every bit of dirt had to be hauled out in wheelbarrows. After many months of arduous labor the dimensions of the hole in the ground corresponded to a competition-size pool. At this stage the administration stepped in. They made a special effort to raise the needed funds and contracted for the completion of the project. The comradeship we felt as we watched the pool fill with water and took our first swim in it must have been similar to the elation of the Jews when they dedicated the wall of Jerusalem. Our common venture, undertaken for the common good, had the effect of binding us together. This feeling of unity gave us a new sense of identity (particularly in competing against other schools!). Our morale was such that we appeared to others to be unbeatable.

In the case of the Israelites, the building of the wall has restored their national prestige. Their awakened spiritual sensitivity has led to a spiritual renewal of a lasting kind. The repopulation of the city of Jerusalem has given them a sense of corporate strength. And now, as they walk around the walls that they have built, sing praises to the glory of God, and offer their thank offerings, they receive a new sense of worth. The result is great God-given joy!

Joy is the absence of anxiety. The joy of the Lord is the secret of our strength (Nehemiah 8:10). We lose our joy when we ex-

perience anxiety. This frequently happens when our behavior
is in conflict with our ideals. Many Christians endure joyless
lives because their practice in the nitty-gritty situations of life
does not conform to what they know God expects of them. As a
consequence they suffer from frustration and face eventual
defeat.

The solution to joylessness is to once again set ourselves
apart to the Lord. Whether we call this consecration, dedication, or sanctification is of little importance. What is important
is that we give Him first place in our lives. When this is done,
the inner reality of our faith will take the place of conformity to
an external set of standards. From this premise, we will be
able to develop true spiritual identity and grow towards
maturity.

The Secret of Strength

With this renewed impetus, the people of Judah take steps to
insure that those who minister to them will be well cared for.
Their concern extends even to the singers and the gatekeepers.
They know that if they are careless and fail to support those
who contribute to their spiritual well-being, they will suffer the
consequences of their neglect (Nehemiah 12:44-47). In addition,
as they continue to learn more of God's will from His Word
(13:1-3), they find it written that Moabites and Ammonites are
to be excluded from the assembly of God (Deuteronomy 23:3-5;
compare Nehemiah 2:19; 13:4). They act in obedience to God's
revealed will and excommunicate them from their number.

The effect of their obedience may be gleaned from the
repetitious use of the word *they* throughout the narrative, the
reminder of their *unity* under David, and the usage of the word
"Israel" in 12:47 and 13:3. Previously there had been an emphasis on the "sons of Benjamin" and the "sons of Judah."
This, however, is now replaced by "Israel." They submit
themselves to a common *authority* (God's Word), share a common *joy*, and have a common *hope* for the future. All of this
regulates their system of values.

The teaching of this passage is not without significance for
us today. When we are right with God, other things will fall into

place. We will delight in those who minister to us in Christ's stead (Nehemiah 12:44b) and count it an honor to see that they are properly supported in their work. We will also have a renewed respect for the Word of God. As we internalize it we will find that its message transforms our lives. It will not only bring us into close contact with reality and give meaning to the here and now; it will also add the dimension of joy to our experience.

Some years ago I was privileged to visit a country church. The congregation had appealed to their denomination for funds to build a sanctuary. Because their minister had not graduated from one of the "approved" schools, their petition was declined. Undaunted by this refusal the members decided to build their own church. They gave sacrificially of their means and spent weekends and vacations laying the foundation. Finally, after many months of labor they were able to begin erecting the walls. Great excitement prevailed when the sanctuary reached windowsill height. Some of the people began speculating that they would be in their church by Christmas. As the building progressed these believers developed a greater oneness than they had ever known before. They began caring for each other and showed, by acts of kindness, a love they never dreamed was possible. Finally, on a never-to-be-forgotten Sunday they held their first service in their new building. The walls had not been painted, and the benches on which they sat left much to be desired. Their joy, however, had to be experienced to be believed. There was a cohesion in this group of believers that I had never experienced anywhere else. Their love for the Lord and for one another caused them to subordinate their own personal desires to the good of the whole. They were a living example of Christianity in action.

As a result of their experiences they became a dynamic force in the community. Outsiders were attracted to the church by the personal joy of the members. They wanted to share the same kind of warmth and fellowship. When they came to find out why these Christians were so different from other Christians they knew, they found a love for one another which was absent elsewhere (see John 13:34-35; 15:12-13,17; 1 John 3:11-23; 4:7-18). It wasn't long before the genuine concern of these believers for them melted any resistance they may have had to the claims of Christ. They were saved and became a part of the same loving, caring, rejoicing community of believers.

TIME FOR REFLECTION

1. Should a Christian plan a definite reading schedule that would include history as well as church history? What rationale would you give for such a practice? What place would you give in your reading schedule to biography? How would you avoid the problems of "hero worship"? What guidance may be gleaned from the general teaching of Scripture on this point?

2. Different people possess different gifts. Nehemiah 12 mentions priests (who officiated inside the temple precincts), Levites (who generally ministered in the more mundane duties associated with the temple), "administrators" of households, gatekeepers, singers, those who played different kinds of musical instruments, etc. What do we learn from this chapter about the use of gifts? Which gifts do you possess (see the lists in Romans 12:6-9; 1 Corinthians 12:4-11; and Ephesians 4:11-16)? How may these gifts of yours be most effectively used?

3. At the dedication of the wall of Jerusalem the different groups of people went through different rituals (for purification purposes). Are there any abiding principles in these rituals?

4. One writer described joy as "perfect acquiescence in God's will because the soul delights itself in God Himself." How would you describe joy? Why is joy generally experienced when we are engaged in "other directed" activities? How will the "joy of the Lord" (Nehemiah 8:10) show itself in a group of believers? What will be the result of this joy?

Something to think about: Chuck Swindoll, radio pastor of *Insight for Living* said:

Leaders need to be happy people! Those who look to a leader for encouragement and hope aren't ready for a personification of the grim reaper. Many of the followers crawl to work every morning whipped black-and-blue by domestic conflicts and a ton of financial worries. They face a day of monotonous demands and thankless tasks, only later to return home to bickering, discontented mates and kids. Away from the job they have little more to look forward to than the glare of the television set. Somewhere, somehow, God can use you to introduce the one ingredient—real lasting joy—that will lighten their load.

17

THE PROBLEM OF PRESERVING FREEDOM

Nehemiah 13:4-31

In concluding his study of the book of Nehemiah, Walter F. Adeney pointed out that if Nehemiah's "Memoirs" had been an historical novel instead of an accurate record of the events, then bringing down the curtain at the end of chapter 12 or with 13:3, would have rounded off the story and brought it to a perfect conclusion. With this kind of ending we all would have rested easily and felt inwardly glad that in one man's experience, at least, there had been a happy resolution of all the many conflicts of life.

Instead of this kind of conclusion there is an "appendix." This appendix proves the wisdom of Thomas Jefferson's now famous observation, "Eternal vigilance is the price of freedom." It also emphasized the continuing need for good leaders.

Backdrop

During the remaining eleven and one-half years of Nehemiah's administration, things run smoothly. The opposition party in Jerusalem can do little to oppose so capable an administrator. Outwardly they conform to the covenant, and the people live relatively prosperous, uneventful lives. However, after more than a decade as governor (444-432 B.C.), Nehemiah returns to the court of Artaxerxes. He remains in Babylon for twelve years. During his absence, the opposition party—made up of the high priest and his family, and the influential citizens of the city—discard Nehemiah's separatist policies in favor of fewer restraints, "open dialogue" with those in Samaria, and the removal of inhibiting influences.

In about 420 B.C., Nehemiah is again appointed governor of Judah. The fact that he asks for permission to return to Jerusalem may indicate that he has some knowledge of conditions in Judah. In any event, he is again sent to the province as the representative of the king.

On his arrival, Nehemiah sees that the Temple and its worship has been forsaken (Nehemiah 13:11; compare 10:39). He looks for the cause and finds it in the *toleration of evil*.

During Nehemiah's previous administration, and as long as he remained in Jerusalem, Eliashib was held in check. But when Nehemiah left for Babylon, the high priest began to engage in a diplomatic role. One of his first moves was to have a member of his family marry into the family of Tobiah. Then, as a token of good will, he took certain of the storage rooms of the Temple—rooms under his direct supervision—and converted them into a penthouse for Tobiah. And Tobiah is an Ammonite (Nehemiah 2:19; Deuteronomy 23:4).

We may be sure that this move did not please the common people. They would have retained some loyalty to Nehemiah. However, even if they were outraged at what Eliashib was doing, they were powerless to oppose him. After all, in the "new" administration, the leaders of Jerusalem were aiming at being conciliatory. Twelve years of "reform," they felt, was long enough. Now was the time, in the interests of their expanding economy, for them to be kind to their enemies. Therefore God's Law was discarded and evil was called by another name.

But Eliashib reckoned without one critic—Malachi. In Nehemiah's absence, the prophet preached against these practices (Malachi 2:1-9). His words were directed largely to the people and went unheeded by the priesthood. There was no one powerful enough to stand against Eliashib.

But what began with the toleration of the presence of Tobiah in the temple area had far-reaching effects on the people. Because storage rooms had been converted into a private apartment, the people no longer gave to the support of the Temple. The Levites, to sustain their families, found it necessary to go back to their farms. With the lapse of spiritual training, the people became lax in practical righteousness. Commercial enterprises began to encroach on the Lord's day, and a decline in morality was the inevitable result.

Bold Reform

On Nehemiah's return to Jerusalem he analyzes the problem, and takes decisive steps to correct it. He enters the temple courts and throws out the furniture of Tobiah. He then gives instructions for the rooms to be cleaned and returned to their original purpose. All this takes courage—the courage of a man whose convictions are firmly established upon the bedrock of Holy Scripture. Significantly, Eliashib does nothing to oppose him. He realizes that in Nehemiah he has met his match.

Nehemiah's success may be attributed to the fact that he acts decisively. Had he convened a meeting of the city fathers, or consulted with his advisors, the cause would have been lost. Instead, considering the general teaching of the Word of God, and remaining within the realm of his authority, he acts with resolute determination.

Men of Nehemiah's ability are sorely needed today. Both in the church and outside of it we have long tolerated error. On the one hand there is false doctrine and a pseudopiety that allows the enemies of the truth to minimize the cardinal tenets of the faith and to control the curricula of our colleges and seminaries; on the other hand, the old principles of morality and integrity have been set aside for policies built upon expediency and the belief that the end justifies the means. These trends in both sacred and secular spheres need to be challenged by those who adhere to and practice the principles of godliness. But the cause of spiritual decline needs to be attacked at the root, where it began, in the toleration of evil.

Facing the Issues

Having taken care of the primary cause of the spiritual decline in Judah, Nehemiah now sets about rectifying the wrongs which have arisen. He finds that the portions for the Levites have not been given to them. In his absence from the

city, Malachi had exhorted the people to bring their tithes into
the storehouse (Malachi 3:7-12). The people, however, had lost
confidence in the priesthood, and were caught up in caring for
their own concerns. As a result, the House of God was forsaken.

When Nehemiah ascertains why the temple services are no
longer being held, he contends with the officials of the city.
After all, they share in the responsibility of running the capital
and have a voice in the affairs of the city. Nehemiah's confrontation with them must have awakened their sense of responsibility. They set about encouraging the Jews to bring in their
tithes and the next verse indicates that the people respond willingly (compare Exodus 30:34; Leviticus 2:1-6; 6:15; 24:7;
Deuteronomy 18:3). Under Nehemiah's strong leadership the
priests and Levites resume their former functions; and
Eliashib's star sets, never to rise again. He is replaced with
reliable men who are selected from the different groups
(Nehemiah 13:13) and charged with the responsibility of making fair and equitable distribution to their kinsmen.

Participation in Evil

The toleration of evil in Jerusalem has also had a damaging
effect on the people in the towns and villages of Judah. When
the Levites were forced to leave the city, spiritual laxity set in.
This apathy fostered a spirit of indifference; the Temple was
neglected and the Sabbath was desecrated.

In the days following his return to Jerusalem, Nehemiah sees
some Jews in the province treading wine presses on the Sabbath. Others are bringing sacks of grain to Jerusalem to be
ready for market the next day. And men from Tyre are actually
holding open market on this holy day.

The observance of the Sabbath had always been a stumbling
block in the way of free trade between pious Jews and their
Gentile neighbors. The temptation to engage in trade with the
people of the nations around them was always present.
Adherence to the Sabbath as the Lord's day was a special
mark of spirituality, particularly in a time of spiritual laxity.

In his handling of the situation, Nehemiah's courage is once more in evidence. He approaches the nobles of the city[1] who have a greater interest in the economy than anyone else, and "contends" with them. "What is this evil that you are doing? . . . Didn't our fathers do the same thing so that God brought on us, and on our city, all this trouble? Yet you are adding to the wrath on Israel by profaning the sabbath."

In speaking to them in this way, Nehemiah gives them a reason for his reprimand, and challenges them with their failure to exercise proper responsibility. He also shows, by means of historic precedent, the dire consequences of their failure to lead the people in the paths of righteousness (see Jeremiah 17:19-27; Ezekiel 20:12-24).

The nobles appear apathetic. Apparently they are unwilling to take decisive action. Nehemiah, therefore, steps in. He commands that the gates of the city be closed before the Sabbath and instructs his servants to see that no merchandise is brought into the city. Once or twice the merchants spend the night outside the city. Some writers believe that the noise they created brought on Nehemiah's warning in verse 19. Others think the Jews may have gone outside the city to trade with the Tyrians (compare Leviticus 23:32; Amos 8:5). Whatever the reason, Nehemiah threatened the merchants with imprisonment if they do this again. They don't! They are overawed by a man of such strong convictions.

Finally, to insure the proper sanctity of the Sabbath, Nehemiah instructs the Levites to dedicate themselves to the task of preserving it. The duty is a sacred one. They are to act as gatekeepers and prevent anyone—Jews or Tyrians—from trading on the Sabbath.

But why restrict the liberty of the Jews? And if it was so important for *them* to keep the Sabbath, why isn't it binding on us today?

The Sabbath was a day of rest. As early as Genesis 2:2, it

[1] The question may validly be asked, What happened to Hanani during Nehemiah's absence? Of the possible answers, two are worthy of consideration. (1) He may have been removed from office by Eliashib or those in league with the high priest soon after Nehemiah left for Babylon. It may also have been a communication from Hanani which brought Nehemiah back to Jerusalem. Or (2) he may have died in the intervening twelve years. No mention is made of Ezra in Nehemiah 13 and the probability is that Ezra had also passed on to his eternal reward.

symbolized cessation from exertion. In ancient Israel, the seventh day of the week, Saturday, was set aside as a "holy" day (Exodus 16:23-29; 20:10-11; 31:17). Work was expressly forbidden (Exodus 35:3; Numbers 15:32). The keeping of the Sabbath was a sign between a covenant-keeping God and His people (Ezekiel 20:12,20). The whole history of the Jewish Sabbath was designed to serve as an illustration for us. It dramatized the spiritual rest into which we may enter when we cease from our own strivings after holiness and rest in the provision God has made for us in Christ (Hebrews 4:4). The reason for the legalistic enforcement of the Sabbath in Old Testament times was to preserve God's "type" intact for us.[2]

Unfortunately for us, the toleration of evil leads to spiritual laxity, and spiritual laxity paves the way for doctrinal indifference, and when this happens we become ignorant of God's provision for us. Our sensitivity to spiritual realities fades, and we have no rational basis for maintaining any semblance of commitment to God. Moral degeneracy then becomes the inevitable result.

Voice of the Siren

Nehemiah's final act of reform is in the area of mixed marriages. As he travels about he finds that Jews have intermarried with women from Ashdod, Ammon, and Moab (see Exodus 34:15-16; Deuteronomy 7:1-4). Apparently, it was a case of the old story of forbidden things being more appealing than those which were regulated for their good (compare Joshua 23:12-13; Malachi 2:11-12).

The consequences of such marriages are illustrated for us in what Nehemiah found. There was corruption in the home. The mothers reared their children in their own pagan ways, and spiritual ignorance prevailed.

The contrast between the kind of home God intended us to have and the type of home that frequently exists where godlessness is found, has been described by Arthur T. Pierson.

---

[2] Those interested in pursuing this theme are recommended to read Dr. W. Graham Scroggie's *The Land of Life and Rest* (London: Pickering and Inglis, n.d.); and Dr. Merrill F. Unger's article on "Sabbath" in *Unger's Bible Dictionary* (1961).

In his book, *The Bible and the Spiritual Life,* Dr. Pierson contrasts two family case histories: the family of Jonathan Edwards and the family of Max Jukes.

Jonathan Edwards was born into a godly home. His father was a preacher, and before him, his mother's father. His descendants were committed to the Word of God and followed principles of honesty and integrity. More than four hundred of them have been traced. They include college presidents, professors, ministers of the gospel, missionaries, theologians, lawyers and judges, and authors of high rank.

A careful research into the history of the criminal family of Max Jukes has shown a long record of prostitution and drunkenness, imbecility and insanity. A total of twelve hundred descendants have been traced of this prolific family tree. A large number were physically self-wrecked. Some were professional paupers, others were convicted criminals, or murderers. Out of the whole twelve hundred, only twenty ever learned a trade and of these, half of them owed it to prison discipline.

The influence of a godly home can further be attested by examining the rearing of people such as F. B. Meyer, W. Graham Scroggie, James Hudson Taylor, John and Charles Wesley, and many others. There is no substitute for a godly home (1 Timothy 4:8)!

In correcting this sorrowful situation, Nehemiah contends with those who have intermarried with women of the surrounding nations. He strikes some of them and pulls out their hair. Then he reprimands them: "You shall not give your daughters to their sons, nor take of their daughters for your sons, or for yourselves. Did not Solomon, king of Israel, sin regarding these things? Yet among the many nations, there was no king like him, and he was loved by his God, and God made him king over Israel; nevertheless the foreign women caused even him to sin. Do we then hear about you that you have committed all this great evil by acting unfaithfully against our God by marrying foreign women?"

Interestingly enough, in acting as he did, Nehemiah cites the condemnation of history. He points to the wisest man of all time and asks in effect, "Do you expect to fare any better than he?"

Not only does intermarriage between a believer and an unbeliever pave the way for corruption in the home, it also strikes at the very basis of marriage. Marriage is regarded as a covenant entered into between two people and God (Proverbs 2:17; Ezekiel 16:8; Malachi 2:14). The home is designed to be the basis of society, the structure upon which the nation is built. Any departure from this ideal can only have a detrimental effect upon all concerned.

In carrying out these reforms, Nehemiah finds that he must again confront the household of the high priest, Eliashib. During his absence in Babylon, the grandson of Eliashib has married the daughter of Sanballat. Special regulations governed the marriage of priests, and particularly one who might one day become the high priest (see Leviticus 21:6-8,13-14; Deuteronomy 23:8-11). Nehemiah takes care of this lawbreaker by rebuking him and "chasing him from his presence." Tradition claims that this man's name was Manasseh, and that when chased out of Nehemiah's presence he went to his father-in-law in Samaria and started a rival form of worship on Mt. Gerizim.[3]

The reform completed, Nehemiah again settles down to a period of relatively tranquil administration. In the leadership which he gives the people, he combines integrity with ability. He is not afraid to act, and his actions are governed by his knowledge of and submission to the Scriptures.

Making Changes

As we look back over the material we have covered, we cannot help but compare this chapter with the signing of the covenant in Nehemiah 10. There the people pledged themselves to maintain the House of God, provide for the priesthood, preserve the Sabbath, and abstain from intermarriage with the heathen. During Nehemiah's first administration, these regulations were adhered to. However, as soon as he left for Babylon, spiritual decline set in.

In comparing the situation of Nehemiah's time with our own, we see that there is a marked parallel. We too need capable leaders! And Nehemiah provides our leaders with an example

---

[3] It was this shrine the woman of Samaria referred to when she said to the Lord Jesus, "Our fathers worshipped in this mountain" (John 4:20). See H. A. Ironside, *Lectures on the Book of Acts* (New York: Loizeaux Bros., 1943), pp.176-185; and Josephus, *Antiquities of the Jews*, XI:8.2,4.

to follow. He was committed to practicing the truth. This gave him a clear understanding of the difference between right and wrong (Hebrews 5:13-14). It also gave him the capacity to take decisive action; when he acted, it was with courage based on conviction.

Secondly, Nehemiah always began by working through existing leaders (see Nehemiah 13:11,17,25). Where the leadership was inadequate, he took steps to replace it with reliable personnel (13:13). When faced with moral apathy and spiritual indifference he exercised righteous indignation.

We are inclined to think of anger as being sinful. The Lord Jesus, however, was angry (Matthew 21:12; Mark 3:5; John 2:15-17), yet without sin (Hebrews 4:15). Great leaders who have turned the tide of national and spiritual decline have likewise been men who could be aroused to anger at the social and moral injustices that were current in their day.

Anger, however, may be abused. It is far too easy for us to excuse our own weakness of character by calling our loss of self-control "righteous indignation." The Apostle Paul knew only too well that we can be led into sin by our anger (Ephesians 4:26-27). Righteous anger, however, is free from selfishness. When Nehemiah "contended" with those who had failed in their duty, or who were guilty of violating God's Law, his conduct should not be looked upon as the action of a man in uncontrollable rage. Instead, as H. E. Ryle has pointed out, he was acting in the capacity of "a public officer in the faithful discharging of his duties." He knew that different situations call for different strategies. Some people will respond to a verbal rebuke. Others need something a little more physical to make them aware of the gravity of the situation. When Nehemiah chased the grandson of the high priest from his presence, he was, in effect, treating an apostate in the manner his conduct deserved.

The Important Connection

But what are we to make of Nehemiah's prayers (Nehemiah 13:14,22b,31)? Are they the last recourse of a despondent old man? Is this all a righteous person, who has devoted his entire life to the good of others, can look forward to?

We make a great mistake if we follow modern commentators and evaluate Nehemiah's prayers in the light of our own discouragements. Anyone who can engage in such vigorous reforms and risk antagonizing not only the high priest and his family but the officials and nobles of Judah as well, is not likely to give way easily to despair.

Despair might result if his efforts were largely unproductive, or if circumstances led Nehemiah to believe that he had failed to live up to his concept of an ideal. But this was not Nehemiah's experience. By seeking God's approval alone he was kept from trying to attain the unattainable.

There seems to be a much better explanation for these prayers. Nehemiah lived his entire life in the presence of the Lord. He was conscious of God's eye upon him, and he did everything with the view of receiving God's approval (compare Ephesians 1:9-14).

It will help us understand the situation if we realize that Nehemiah was nearly at the end of his earthly pilgrimage. How long he continued as governor is uncertain. His prayers give evidence of the fact that he knew his bodily vigor was not what it used to be. This is why he prays that God will have compassion on him and strengthen him. In addition, he was looking beyond the temporal scene to the one that awaited him. And so he prays, "Remember me, O my God, for good." As with the Apostle Paul, he labored unceasingly with the view of meriting God's approval (Philippians 3:12-16), and desired only that his work on earth might earn him the kind of rewards that would last for eternity.

When All Is Said and Done

In the final analysis, Nehemiah's life and ministry point to the fact that we all need capable leadership. Without it, we are like sheep having no shepherd. In the absence of godly leaders, moral and spiritual decline sets in and the result is the destruction of our national and spiritual heritage. Political freedom is based on spiritual freedom. When spiritual freedom is sacrificed through the toleration of evil, it inevitably results in oppression and the demise of moral standards.

To counteract these trends, we need a return to the Word of

God (see Nehemiah 8). Then, by submitting ourselves to it, and confessing our failures and shortcomings, we can begin to walk in a path of obedience, righteousness, and true holiness. Out of a spirit of genuine renewal there will come spiritual, social, and national freedom.

TIME FOR REFLECTION

1. The first area in which Nehemiah instituted reform concerned the cleansing of the temple. As a discerning leader, he went to the source of the problem (Nehemiah 13:7). Why did he institute such seemingly harsh measures in dispossessing Tobiah of his "apartment"?

   During Nehemiah's absence, Malachi had rebuked the priests (Malachi 1:6-8). Why had they ignored his counsel? What happens to laymen in our churches when those in the ministry openly practice compromise?

2. The second area of reform concerned the Levites. When their support from the temple failed, they went back to their farms. Why did Nehemiah approach the officials about this retreat? Were the officials under an obligation to see that the temple ministries were maintained (see Nehemiah 10:39b)? What should they have done?

   During Nehemiah's stay in Babylon, Malachi had reproved and exhorted the people (Malachi 3:8-10). Why had the majority paid little attention to him? What administrative breakdown made it difficult for them to follow his admonition? What is the result in our time when those chosen by God to minister to us are insufficiently supported?

3. The third area of Nehemiah's reform concerned the sabbath. Whom did Nehemiah confront? What measures did he institute? How successful was he? Why was the observance of the sabbath important to the Jews (see Exodus 20:8-11; Jeremiah 17:21-27; Ezekiel 20:12,20)? Of what significance is the "sabbath rest" to believers today (see Hebrews 3:11b; 4:1)?

4. The final act of Nehemiah's reform concerned mixed marriages (a) on the part of the people (Nehemiah 13:23-27) and (b) on the part of the high priest's son (13:28). Did Nehemiah act in accordance with Scripture in insisting that these people divorce their wives (compare Exodus 34:15-16; Deuteronomy 7:1-4)? What had Malachi taught about mixed marriages (Malachi 2:10-12)? Why did Nehemiah deal so forcefully

with the son of the high priest (compare Leviticus 2:6-8,14-15; Malachi 2:4-9)?

What happens in homes today when a Christian marries a non-Christian believing that he (or she) will later win the spouse to the Lord? What is the effect on them and their children?

5. In Nehemiah 13, what are the different ways in which Nehemiah dealt with different attitudes on the part of the officials and the people? What do his dealings indicate about his leadership?

Something to think about: Dr. A. W. Tozer, in *The Next Chapter After the Last*, observed:

Time may show that one of the greatest weaknesses in our modern civilization has been the acceptance of quantity rather than quality as the goal after which we strive.

18

PROFILE OF A LEADER

As we review the material contained in these chapters, it
will be of help to us if we enlarge upon our previous threefold
outline. By giving each chapter a title and then grouping certain chapters together (e.g., 4—6 and 8—10) we will see clearly
the main movements in the book.

A SURVEY OF NEHEMIAH

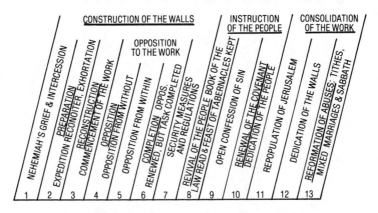

In our review we will concentrate on the personal
characteristics of an effective leader, and the basic principles
of sound leadership. These two facets constitute *the dynamics
of effective leadership;* and Nehemiah provides an important
"case history" for our study of both of them.

The Personal Characteristics of
an Effective Leader

First, an effective leader must be a man of *integrity*. He must possess uprightness of character and soundness of moral principles. He must know and stand for what is right—even in the face of popular disfavor. Only then will he have the inner dynamic which will inspire others to follow him with confidence.

But how is integrity developed? Nehemiah shows us that it comes from a commitment to the Word of God. Nehemiah's prayers (see Nehemiah 1:5-11, etc.) are permeated with quotations from Scripture. His life and reforms show us that he ordered his conduct in accordance with God's revealed will (5:9-12,14-19; 10:1,32-39; 13:4-28). And he expected those under him to follow the same principles of honesty and integrity.

Stemming from a basic commitment to live under the authority of Holy Writ is *conviction*.

Conviction has as its foundation our faith in God, and faith forms the basis of our confidence in ourselves, the courage with which we face our opposition, and our dedication to the task at hand. Without this kind of conviction there can be no lasting accomplishment.

Nehemiah's convictions may be seen in his confidence that God would answer his prayer (Nehemiah 1:11), his self-assurance as he replied to his adversaries (2:19-20), the courage and determination with which he handled opposition (4:1-23; 6:1-14), and his persistence when the workers had decided to walk off the job (4:10-11).

A logical corollary of conviction is *loyalty*—loyalty to the Lord, loyalty to our superiors, and loyalty to those in our congregations or places of business who look to us for leadership and guidance. Without loyalty we fall prey to compromises and are characterized by indecision when we should act decisively. When this happens our church members or subordinates become confused and the end result is the undermining of our leadership.

Nehemiah's loyalty to the Lord was unquestioned. And his loyalty to Artaxerxes was no less real (Nehemiah 2:3). It provided the *only* sure foundation in a time of crisis (2:1-8). Without proven loyalty to back up his words, his cause would have been lost. The king would not have had confidence in him and Nehemiah might never have regained his position of influence at court.

With loyalty goes *stability*. Stability is more than showing our reliability under pressure. It includes a willingness to accept responsibility, take the initiative, and persevere with a task until it is finished. A loser is one who encounters opposition and doesn't have the courage to press on. He then fabricates a "reason" for his failure and is forever destined to mediocrity. A leader, on the other hand, is one who has the capacity to dominate and finally to master the circumstances that surround him.

In contrast to the loser, there is the example of Nehemiah. He accepted a new responsibility (Nehemiah 2:6b), and began a task many believed to be impossible. He showed himself dependable under pressure (4—6) and saw the entire project through to a successful conclusion.

In addition, the leader who puts God first in his life and is loyal to his employer, will more than likely have a real *concern for others*. His unselfishness will lead him to treat fairly those who work with him. He will seek their personal advancement, and will put their well-being ahead of his own. And they will respond with work which is qualitatively and quantitatively better.

Nehemiah was concerned for the Jews (Nehemiah 1:4-11; 5:1-5; 13:18). He identified himself with the people. The people felt that he was approachable. As a result, the dynamic of his own personality inspired them. He did not dominate them as the other governors had done. And they responded to his leadership by persevering with the work.

A leader whose dedication to the task at hand is balanced by his concern for others, will be able to view the whole project— the work and the workers—with proper *discernment*. This perspective is vital if his decisions are to be just and equitable; only with proper discernment can he act decisively. Of course, discernment involves a knowledge of the facts, an awareness of what needs to be done, and the development of a plan of action designed to achieve the desired results.

Nehemiah was a man of keen discernment. He knew what needed to be done (Nehemiah 2:5) and he augmented his knowledge with additional firsthand data (2:12-15). He not only dealt in concepts, but possessed the ability to master details as well. Then, on the basis of his evaluation of the men and the resources, he set a goal (2:17). The establishing of a definite objective automatically ordered his priorities.

When we have a basic commitment to the Lord, are loyal to our superiors, and treat our subordinates as people instead of things, we will find it relatively simple to motivate others. *Motivation* is linked with enthusiasm. Our dedication to the task we have undertaken will make us enthusiastic about what we are doing. It will provide us with a sense of direction. This makes motivation easy.

Nehemiah had no difficulty motivating people (Nehemiah 2:17-18). He challenged them with what needed to be done, encouraged them with the benefits they would derive from rebuilding the wall, and gave them proof of God's involvement with the work. The result was an enthusiastic response!

Finally, there is *tact*—the ability to deal with others without creating offense. Tact involves the knack of saying and doing the right thing in the right way at the right time and in the right place. It involves having an intimate understanding of human nature and a genuine concern for the feelings of others.

On one occasion I was asked to serve as a consultant for a library to be built on the campus of a midwestern college. In the initial interview, I found the architect to be so agreeable I was convinced that working with him would be a pleasure. In the course of time, however, I found that in committee when his views conflicted with those of the college librarian, he would invariably say, "Well, men, I agree with you in principle." It took me a little while to realize that he had not the slightest intention of putting into practice the things which he appeared to be committed to in principle. His congenial manner was used to delude people into thinking that he was in agreement with them. *His tact was not founded on truth.* The result was an inevitable confrontation . . . with all of its accompanying unpleasantness!

Nehemiah possessed the ability to be tactful (Nehemiah 2:5-8). His tact, however, was grounded upon his personal integrity and his felt concern for the feelings of others. With definite convictions forming the basis of his philosophy of life, he could seek the best method of dealing with each situation. The result was a discreet blending of truth and grace. In the decision he reached and the action he took, there was no compromise or deceit.

Those of us who wish to improve our leadership skills have Nehemiah as an example. We can probe the springs of his life, emulate his integrity, learn from his convictions, develop the same sense of loyalty, understand the basic dynamics of motivation, and exercise the same tactfulness. As we develop these personal characteristics, we will grow in stature as leaders.

The Basic Principles of Sound Leadership

In defining the basic principles of good leadership, one nationally prominent corporation president said: "In choosing a capable executive, I look first for intellectual ability. I think that comes above almost anything else. Next I look for a kind of leadership stature. I hope the man looks like a leader and has some ability to command attention just by his sheer presence and force of personality. Then I hope this is balanced with some humility. There is nothing worse than somone who has great intellectual power and, at the same time, is arrogant." But is this all? The late President Eisenhower exposed the fallacy of having an inadequate idea of what is involved in leadership. "A quality common to leaders is their willingness to work hard, to prepare themselves, and to know their field of activity thoroughly. I have heard it said of some individuals: 'Oh, he'll get by on his personality.' Well, he may 'get by' for a time, but if a charming personality is all he has, the day will come when he will find himself looking for a job."

Let us see if we can analyze the basic principles of sound leadership. Whereas many Christian institutions choose leaders on the basis of their appearance or personality, academic qualifications or connections, there are other criteria that merit our consideration.

In considering the case of Nehemiah, we find that he was *knowledgeable*. He obtained as much information from Hanani as possible (Nehemiah 1:2; 2:8). He may even have visited a building project while still in Susa. If so, he would have observed some construction in progress.[1] He certainly knew what he required before the king asked about his needs (2:8), and he enlarged upon his knowledge (2:12-15).

A thorough knowledge of our task is a basic prerequisite to competent leadership. There is, however, also the need to know ourselves. We need to engage in continuous self-evaluation, be aware of our strengths as well as our weaknesses, and constantly strive for self-improvement. The moment we stop learning, we stop growing. When this happens, we can no longer take the initiative, we lose confidence in ourselves, and our subordinates soon find this out. The inevitable result is that before long our administration is labeled "incompetent." I have known business executives, mission board superintendents, and pastors of whom this was tragically true.

While an intimate knowledge of ourselves is indispensable to sound leadership, so is a thorough knowledge of those with whom we work. We should know our employees and be concerned for their welfare. In an unsigned editorial in *Supervisory Management* the writer said, "A basic function of a good leader is to inspire people to their best efforts. The man who concentrates only on details, on cost figures, or on technical matters, may become an expert, but not a leader. Experts know what should be done; leaders know what should be done and *how to get people to do it.*"

Nehemiah was concerned about those who worked with him (Nehemiah 3; 5:1-13). He paid close attention to details (see Nehemiah 8:10-12), and also knew how to build and sustain their *morale.*

Many "task specialists" find it easy to build the morale of their employees, but experience difficulty maintaining it. They have little success in developing proper *esprit de corps*—the unity of purpose, loyalty to, pride in, and enthusiasm for their

[1] The palace at Susa had been built by Darius I, but enlarged and embellished by later kings. It is highly probable that Nehemiah had observed this or some other building in the course of erection or modification. In any event, he had ample opportunity to learn from the master builders of Babylon some of the techniques that would have been of help to him when he engaged in rebuilding the wall of Jerusalem.

church, or department, and its work—and as a result morale
sags. Proper morale can be built only by knowing what makes
our employees "tick." When we know how to motivate them,
we can enthuse them with our own personal dynamic, encourage them with the task that needs to be done, and
challenge them with the satisfaction of accomplishment.

Also of importance in maintaining morale is the proper
dissemination of information. People want to know what is going on around them, and the part they are to play in the plans of
the administration. They also want to know how the administration views them as a group, and whether or not their
work is appreciated. The same is true of individuals. Wise
managers will keep these things in mind, insure that the channels of communication are kept open, make sure that the
workers are encouraged to give of their best, and give some indication of the administration's appreciation of their efforts.

As a wise leader, Nehemiah gave praise where it was due
(Nehemiah 3:20,27,30). He made his decisions known through
subordinates (13:9,14,21,22, etc.). Communication was through
regularly constituted and clearly recognized channels.

Whereas small churches or companies will not need such an
elaborate arrangement, large churches and corporations do.
Well-informed employees serve better when they understand
what is going on around them. They have a comprehensive
view of the whole operation, and know their part in it. They can
then identify with the objectives of their church, mission, or
company, and understand why certain matters are given
priority. They will also know how certain goals are to be
reached. With this understanding, the individual will be able to
establish his personal identity and adjust his behavior to obtain
these corporate ends. In our churches or chosen professions,
as in sports, it is necessary for a person to subordinate his personal desires or ambitions to the best interests of his "team."
Objectives are reached when all concerned are pulling
together. With success comes the pride of accomplishment and
the maintenance of proper *esprit de corps*.

Nehemiah developed a proper team spirit in an admirable
way. He welded more than forty different groups into a unit
(Nehemiah 3). They worked together with proper cooperation,
with each group either complementing or supplementing the

strengths or weaknesses of the other groups. Nehemiah could supervise these groups without giving the workers the idea that they were being "policed." His kindly concern for them made working for him easy. When the work was done, *they* rejoiced in what *they* had accomplished (Nehemiah 12:27-43). They felt that they were an integral part of what had taken place.

All leaders are expected to *set goals*. Progress toward these goals must be steady and persistent. In building the wall of Jerusalem, Nehemiah began with a chaotic situation (Nehemiah 2:17). As the work went forward, he took inventory of their progress (4:6; 6:1). He kept in close touch with the different groups. Evidence of his continued ability to motivate the builders may be seen in the fact that *the people had a mind to work*. When all the doors had been placed in position, he could record the successful completion of their first goal (6:15). He then moved forward toward his second objective—an objective which had already begun to take shape in his mind—the consolidation of the work.

In the final analysis, a leader must lead by *example*. This takes dedication, stamina, courage, fairness, honesty, patience, and persistence. Once again, Nehemiah is in the forefront setting us an example (Nehemiah 4:23; 5:14-18). He was not greedy for possessions (6:6-7; 7:2), nor was he anxious about prestige and the splendor of his court. He set an example of godliness (8:9-10; 10:1; 12:31ff; 13:4-29) for others to emulate.

Possessed of these qualities, it is not surprising that Nehemiah was an effective leader. His "Memoirs" explain to us the dynamics of success! God graciously included them in the canon of Holy Scripture so that we might have a model to follow.

TIME FOR REFLECTION

1. On page 218 you will find a chart. As you reread Nehemiah's memoirs, give a brief descriptive heading to each chapter. No two people see things exactly the same way, and your titles will better fit your needs.

2. As you review the content of the book of Nehemiah, concentrate on the specifics of each chapter (e.g., prayer, ethics, interpersonal relationships, leadership skills, etc.). Insert the appropriate verse(s) in the space provided in the chart. This will help you when you are asked to give a devotional talk to a Sunday school group or gathering of Christians in another setting.

3. Imagine that you have been asked to speak to some business people at a weekend conference. You will address them once on Friday evening, twice on Saturday, and once on Sunday morning. You decide to base your addresses and the subsequent discussion on what may be found in the book of Nehemiah on . . .

   A. *Planning.* To do this you will begin by noting the references to Nehemiah's obtaining reliable information, the way he developed his strategy, established certain objectives, determined his priorities, outlined a program, scheduled the needed supplies, budgeted for the costs, established procedures, and developed policies.
   Set as an objective the development of this message. Give yourself two weeks in which to complete it. Then begin working on the second one.

   B. *Organizing.* Focus on Nehemiah's organizational skills in Nehemiah 3. Consider how he delegated authority—how much and to whom. All of this will have a bearing on the organizational strategy he used.

   C. *Leading.* This involves decision-making, communication, motivation, selection of personnel for key positions, and the development of capable subordinates.

D. *Controlling.* This is accomplished through the establishing of performance standards, the measuring of production, the evaluation of the progress of the work, correcting what is wrong, commending honest effort, and the reevaluating of goals and objectives.

In all of these areas Nehemiah will be found to be an admirable leader.

	1	2	3	4	5	6	7	8	9	10	11	12	13
Prayer	4-11												
Interpersonal relations													
Leadership or Management Skills													
Emotion(s)	4												
Godward orientation	5ff.												
Knowledge of Scripture	8-10												
Special Concerns	2												
Nehemiah's example and/or ethics													
Personal references	1-2, 4ff.,11												
Problems, (Opposition, etc.)													
Other													

SELECT BIBLIOGRAPHY

Adams, Arthur Merrihew. *Pastoral Administration.* Philadelphia: Westminster Press, 1964.

Albers, Henry. *Principles of Management.* 4th ed. New York: J. Wiley & Sons, 1974.

Alexander, John W. *Managing Your Work.* Downers Grove, Illinois: InterVarsity Press, 1973.

Anderson, Martin. *A Guide to Church Building and Fund Raising.* Minneapolis: Augsburg Press, 1959.

Argyris, Chris. *Integrating the Individual and the Organization.* New York: J. Wiley & Sons, 1964.

_____. *Intervention Theory and Method.* Reading, Massachusetts: Addison-Wesley Publishing Co., 1970.

Atkinson, Charles Harry. *How to Finance Your Church Building Program.* Westwood, New Jersey: Fleming H. Revell Co., 1963.

Barber, Cyril J. *The Minister's Library.* Grand Rapids: Baker Book House, 1974. (Pages 309-330 contain an annotated bibliography covering all phases of leadership and administration).

Bassett, Glenn A. *Management Styles in Transition.* New York: American Management Association, 1966.

Berkman, Harold W. *The Human Relations of Management.* Encino, California: Dickenson Publishing Co., 1974.

Bittel, Lester R. *Management by Exception.* New York: McGraw-Hill Book Co., 1964.

Bower, Marvin. *The Will to Manage.* New York: McGraw-Hill Book Co., 1966.

Bramer, John C., Jr. *Efficient Church Business Management.* Philadelphia: Westminster Press, 1960.

Bursk, Edward C., ed. *Human Relations for Management.* Freeport, New York: Books for Libraries Press, 1972.

Campbell, John P., *et. al. Managerial Behavior, Performance, and Effectiveness.* New York: McGraw-Hill Book Co., 1970.

Carlisle, Howard M. *Situational Management.* New York: Amacom, 1973.

Cashman, Robert. *The Business Administration of a Church.* New York: Harper & Brothers, 1937.

Dalton, Melville. *Men Who Manage.* New York: J. Wiley & Sons, 1966.

Davis, Keith. *The Dynamics of Organizational Behavior.* 3d ed. New York: McGraw-Hill Book Co., 1967.

Ditzen, Lowell R. *Handbook of Church Administration.* New York: Macmillan Co., 1962.

Drucker, Peter Ferdinand. *The Effective Executive.* New York: Harper & Row, 1967.

_____. *Management: Tasks, Responsibilities, Practices.* New York: Harper & Row, 1974.

_____. *Managing for Results.* New York: Harper & Row, 1964.

_____. *The Practice of Management.* New York: Harper & Row, 1954.

Dubin, Robert. *Human Relations in Administration.* 4th ed. Englewood Cliffs, New Jersey: Prentice-Hall, 1973.

Engstrom, Theodore Wilhelm and Alec Mackenzie. *Managing Your Time.* Grand Rapids: Zondervan Publishing House, 1968.

Ewing, David W. *The Human Side of Planning.* London: Collier-Macmillan, 1969.

Fiedler, Fred E. *A Theory of Leadership Effectiveness.* New York: McGraw-Hill Book Co., 1967.

For Executives Only. Chicago: Dartnell Corporation, 1967.

For Those Who Must Lead. By the Faculty, Hillsdale College, Michigan. Chicago: Dartnell Corporation, 1966.

Ford, George L. *Manual on Management for Christian Workers.* Grand Rapids: Zondervan Publishing House, 1964.

Gellerman, Saul W. *Management by Motivation.* New York: American Management Association, 1968.

_____. *The Uses of Psychology in Management.* London: Collier-Macmillan, 1960.

Goble, Frank. *Excellence in Leadership.* New York: American Management Association, 1972.

Gordon, Thomas. *Group-Centered Leadership.* New York: Macmillan Co., 1966.

Hacon, Richard, ed. *Personal and Organizational Effectiveness.* London: McGraw-Hill Book Co., 1972.

Hague, Hawdon. *Executive Self-Development.* New York: J. Wiley & Sons, 1974.

Haire, Mason. *Psychology in Management.* 2d ed. New York: McGraw-Hill Book Co., 1964.

Harral, Stewart. *Public Relations for Churches.* Nashville: Abingdon-Cokesbury Press, 1945.

Heller, Robert. *The Great Executive Dream.* New York: Delacorte Press, 1972.

Hodgetts, Richard M. and Henry H. Albers. *Cases and Incidents on the Basic Concepts of Management.* New York: J. Wiley & Sons, 1972.

Holt, David R. *Handbook of Church Finances.* New York: Macmillan Co., 1960.

Hughes, Charles L. *Goal Setting.* New York: American Management Association, 1965.

Jennings, Eugene E. *An Anatomy of Leadership.* New York: McGraw-Hill Book Co., 1960.

_____. *The Executive in Crisis.* New York: McGraw-Hill Book Co., 1965.

Knowles, Malcolm Shepherd and Hulda F. Knowles. *How to Develop Better Leaders.* New York: Association Press, 1955.

Laird, Donald Anderson and Eleanor C. Laird. *The Techniques of Delegating.* New York: McGraw-Hill Book Co., 1957.

Leach, William H. *Handbook of Church Management.* Englewood Cliffs, New Jersey: Prentice-Hall, 1958.

_____. *Toward a More Efficient Church.* New York: Fleming H. Revell Co., 1948.

Leavitt, Harold J. *Managerial Psychology.* 2d ed. Chicago: University of Chicago Press, 1964.

LeTourneau, Richard. *Management Plus.* Grand Rapids: Zondervan Publishing House, 1973.

Likert, Rensis. *New Patterns of Management.* New York: McGraw-Hill Book Co., 1961.

Lindgren, Alvin J. *Foundations for Purposeful Church Administration.* Nashville: Abingdon Press, 1965.

McLaughlin, Raymond W. *Communication for the Church.* Grand Rapids: Zondervan Publishing House, 1968.

Montgomery, Bernard Law. *The Path to Leadership.* London: Collins Press, 1961.

Odeirne, George S. *Management by Objective.* New York: Pitman, 1965.

Peter, Laurence J. and Raymond Hull. *The Peter Principle.* New York: Morrow & Co., 1969.

Pigours, Paul and Charles A. Myers. *Personnel Administration.* New York: McGraw-Hill Book Co., 1973.

Richardson, Lovella Stoll. *Handbook for the Church Office.* Cincinnati, Ohio: Standard Publishing Co., 1972.

Roethlisberger, F. J. *Management and Morale.* Cambridge: Harvard University Press, 1941.

Rosenberg, Seymour L. *Self-Analysis of Your Organization.* New York: Amacom, 1974.

Salstonstall, Robert, *Human Relations in Administration.* New York: McGraw-Hill Book Co., 1959.

Schaller, Lyle E. and Charles A. Tidwell. *Creative Church Administration.* Nashville: Abingdon Press, 1975.

Schein, Edgar H. *Organization Psychology.* 2d ed. Englewood Cliffs, New Jersey: Prentice-Hall, 1970.

Selznick, Philip. *Leadership in Administration.* New York: Harper & Row, 1957.

Sikula, Andrew F. *Management and Administration.* Columbus, Ohio: Charles E. Merrill Publishing Co., 1973.

Simon, Herbert A. *Administrative Behavior.* New York: Macmillan Co., 1970.

Southard, Samuel. *Ethics for Executives.* New York: Thomas Nelson, 1975.

Stogdill, Ralph M. *Handbook on Leadership.* New York: The Free Press, 1974.

Stoody, Ralph. *A Handbook of Church Public Relations.* Nashville: Abingdon Press, 1959.

Sweet, Herman J. *The Multiple Staff in the Local Church.* Philadelphia: Westminster Press, 1963.

Tannenbaum, R., I. R. Weschler, and F. Massarik. *Leadership and Organization*. New York: McGraw-Hill Book Co., 1961.

Tead, Ordway. *The Art of Leadership*. New York: McGraw-Hill Book Co., 1935.

Wedel, Leonard E. *Building and Maintaining a Church Staff*. Nashville: Broadman Press, 1966.

ACKNOWLEDGMENTS

We gratefully acknowledge permission to quote copyrighted material from these sources:

Airline Management and Marketing: November/December 1971 issue.

American Management Association: J. D. Batten's *Tough-Minded Management*.

Christian Herald: "Life Must Be Faced Squarely," December 1969.

Harvard Business Review: "The Purpose of Business is Not to Make a Profit," April 1973; and "The Pygmalion in Management," July/August 1969.

Macmillan Publishing Company, Inc.: for permission to adapt the maps on pages 48 and 117 from *Macmillan Bible Atlas*, rev. ed., by Yohanan Aharoni and Michael Avi-Yonah, copyright © 1964, 1966, 1968, 1977 by Carta Ltd.

Moody Press: *Toward a Biblical View of Civil Government* by Robert Duncan Culver.

Nation's Business: the March 1970 interview with Walter Finke.

Dr. Charles R. Swindoll: quote from his book *Hand Me Another Brick*.